QANON

How the Deep State Control Your Mind. The Battle Against Conspiracy Theory. The

New World Order; Illuminati Hijacked The World. The Great Awakening! The Story Behind Trump, Obama and others

and entertainment purposes only. All effort has been executed to present accurate, up to date, and reliable, complete information. No warranties of any kind are declared or implied. Readers acknowledge that the author is not engaging in the rendering of legal, financial, medical or professional advice. The content within this book has been derived from various sources. Please consult a licensed professional before attempting any techniques outlined in this book.

By reading this document, the reader agrees that under no circumstances is the author responsible for any losses, direct or indirect, which are incurred as a result of the use of information contained within this document, including, but not limited to, — errors, omissions, or inaccuracies.

Table of Contents

Introduction

What if I told you that modern media could not be trusted? What if you were told that mainstream media is bought out to keep you in the dark to keep you complacent? Would you believe that you are being controlled by people in the shadows who seek to take over everything? Would you believe that you are being lied to and that the truth is there if you look for it?

More and more, people are becoming enlightened—they are red-pilling themselves, as those on the internet commonly say. They recognize that the media is not actually working in the best interest of the people, and they can see that it is imperative that they do something to prevent it. They see that the only real choice here is that they take action. When the government is as corrupt as it is, there is only one right choice, and that choice is the one to take control of the situation. You must do something, and you will need to know how to do it. You must be willing to see that the world is not what it seems and open your eyes.

Qanon is an anonymous poster on the internet that is ready to go out of their way to show the world the truth. Who Q remains a mystery, but we know one thing: He is someone that is vastly powerful. He is someone that is capable of making major changes—of creating situations in which he is going to directly and strongly influence those around him. It is clear that he is someone that is driven to change up everything—to attack the misinformation that goes out and to awaken people to the truth.

What truth, you may ask?

Simple.

The world is being controlled by people who want to take it over. They are a group of super-elites that work together, pulling all of the strings and working to create a government system that is global. They are advocating for a brand new world order—a situation in which they are the only ones that are capable of becoming in control. They want to control it all—to subvert all other governments and maintain authority over the global community.

To some, this might sound like a far-fetched pipe dream. To others, it sounds plausible. To others, it is the truth. This is where Q comes in.

According to Q, Donald Trump is the one thing standing between humanity and being taken over. President Trump is the one reason that we are safe in this world. He is one of the only things standing between us and total destruction and dismantling of the United States.

Of course, the other side does not want you to know the truth—they do not want you to be hesitant or to feel like you should fight back. They want you to trust the media, and they want you to be good little sheep that do as you are told without any expectation of anything else. They want you to be complacent because complacency is easy to control.

Within this book, we are here to delve into the amazing, mysterious, and frightening world of Qanon. We will be taking a closer look at what the theories of Qanon are and how people, the followers of Q, have come to believe that they are true. Through this, you can start to see the truth: That Q is someone that must be heard. You will see that Q may be telling the truth—that it is possible that everything that he has said will actually come to fruition if you listen to what he has to say.

We will go over several key points as you read through this book—we will begin with an introduction to Qanon theory and the background information that you will need to know. We will discuss what the New World order is, as well as how President Trump plays into everything. We will discuss the key players in Q's game, as well as how you can decode what Q posts when he does comment online. We will go over ObamaGate, as well as the idea that the Obama administration, as well as the Democratic National Party, are really just part of the cabal dead set on taking over the world. We will go over how Q has been related to the elections, as well as how he may have been involved. We will take a look at the Great Awakening—the commonly accepted end goal of Q's actions. And finally, we will take a look at the reach that Q has around the world.

Keep in mind that as you read this, Q is currently unknown. As of late 2020, we still do not know who Q is or why he is posting what he is, other than the fact that he is trying to bring enlightenment to us all. No matter whether you are a believer, a doubter, or someone who is not sure what to think of Qanon, this book is for you. As you read through this book, you will be granted information that will help you to see the truth: That Q is out there and that he is acting in a way that is meant to help us all. You will see that he is there for us, helping to keep hope and telling us that we are not alone. He informs us that we are safe, that they are working for us around the clock to protect us, and that tyranny and corruption will fall.

Now, if you are ready to delve into the world of Qanon, we can begin.

Chapter 1: Where We Go One, We Go All: An Intro to Qanon

On the internet, you can find out just about anything. You can find people who believe that the earth is flat. There are people who believe that the world is ruled by lizard people. And, there are the Qanon followers. Often disregarded with the rest of the fringe theory conspiracy theorists, the Qanon followers tend to be referred to by the mainstream media as somewhat unhinged. They are painted out to be these terrible terrorists who are only out for one thing: Destroying democracy.

However, there is more to it than that. As with all good stories, there are more sides to it. Little is known about Q, the mysterious poster on the internet. We don't know who he or she is, but it is commonly accepted that it is a male. He posts online sporadically before disappearing, and sometimes, his posts directly correlate with what you can expect to see from others online. If you have been watching the news, you would know that the United States is full of conflict right now.

According to Q, this is intentional. This is part of the plan to control the world.

Within this chapter, we are going to go through the introduction to Qanon. It all began on a forum on the internet known as 4chan, and from there, it has grown significantly. It all began in October of 2017. From there, Q has become an active poster on the internet. He has a very important role that he has played, and when you stop to look at his actions, his posts, and the choices that he makes, you start to see that there are some patterns.

4chan, 8chan, and 8kun

4chan is an infamous website online in which the expectation is that everyone remains anonymous. This board website is meant to allow people to discuss just anything, all under anonymity, due to the fact that no one is required to register for an account. 4chan, especially among certain boards, is notorious for having people speak to each other with incredibly derogatory language on a regular basis. It is meant to be exclusionary—the idea is that through this exclusionary language, it would be possible to leave certain types of people out—certain types of people are simply not going to be so willing to read it. The vulgarity is meant to weed people out. It is meant to make people not want to be there if they are not willing to take on the language.

Of course, there are some boards that are less vulgar. In particular, on 4chan, /pol/, short for "politically incorrect," is where our story begins. On /pol/, people speak about all things political. Often, the positions taken are less mainstream—they are the thoughts and opinions of those who might be more conservative. On this board, Q began. Now, though Q is no longer present on /pol/, he is still readily and regularly discussed. If you were to visit 4chan's /pol/ board today, you would likely find some Q-specific posts with people discussing the latest Q drops. They "bake bread" with Q's crumbs that are given—they work to decipher the messages that are posted.

Eventually, Q moved to 8chan, a board that was even less regulated than 4chan.

Frederick Brenan, the creator of 8chan, believed that 4chan was growing to become authoritarian in nature and created 8chan as a "free-speech-friendly" alternative. It is somewhere that allows for freedom from regulation. In particular, 8chan had just one rule: Do not post, request, or link to content that would be illegal in the United States. Beyond that, anything goes. Over time, 8chan became known as 8kun during one of many servers, and it now hosts Q's posts as well as a collection of people who want to discuss who Q is and what he does.

Q, as you will come to realize, is something that has been primarily silenced across the internet. The mainstream media and social media sources are trying their hardest to silence the followers, hoping that it would dissolve and lose traction. However, there is one question that must be asked: Why is it that the media would be so driven to silence Q if it were something that should not be concerned about? If Q is nothing but a conspiracy theory, why does the internet want him silenced? Why are people calling for him to be silenced if he is no one to be concerned about? This does not make sense at all—if he is genuinely just some live-action role-player (LARPer) online, why should anyone be frustrated about him? Why should anyone be afraid of him? Why should they try to silence him? All across the internet, fringe theories are allowed to run rampant—no one is silencing the flat earthers beyond just mocking them. No one is telling the lizard people theorists that they have to stop posting or risk being deemed a terrorist organization. The Qanon followers face scrutiny from all sides. They face people from all ends telling them that they cannot congregate, that they cannot discuss their beliefs or thoughts, and that anything pertaining to them will be removed from the internet shortly after being posted.

With the censorship of the internet, places like 4chan and 8kun remain among the few remaining bastions where people can discuss such theories without risking their information being removed. They are among the remaining places that free speech actually means freedom to discuss thoughts that are had. They are some of the remaining areas where people can discuss what matters to them without fear of being shut down or told that they are not allowed that contact with each other.

The Importance of Q

Q is far more important than you may initially believe. The truth is, Q has a singular purpose—getting the truth out. Q wants to enlighten the world—to tell the world and everyone in it what the truth is. He is seeking to reveal a particularly violent, unpleasant truth: That the world is being run by a chain of satanic pedophiles running their own global child sex-trafficking ring with the purpose being to take over the world. They take children, according to Q and the followers who have been dutifully following in his footsteps to put together everything, bit by bit. They were able to follow the breadcrumbs to figure out what it was that Q was telling them.

According to Q, President Donald Trump holds a position that he should not be. He and his administration should not be in power at the moment—the fact that he won alone was something of a miracle according to these people—it was never meant to be. However, it has happened, and it is time to face it—he is there and for a good reason. Q asserts that he is there to fight against corruption. He is draining the swamp of democratic corruption that permeates the US government so we can live safely.

When asked of Q, especially in recent days, President Trump says he does not know much about the movement—he claims that he is unrelated and that he is indifferent, but that he knows that those who are followers of Q are individuals who love the US very much and are working to defend the world.

Q asserts that a day of reckoning is upon us—that sometime in the near future, it will be the case that all of the corruption will be revealed, and those who fought against it will be unable to deny its existence. It will be the case than in that moment that the world will know the truth—that the hidden messages will be revealed and those who were involved in the corruption, such as former presidential candidate Hillary Clinton, will be detained, and possibly even executed. According to Q and his followers, those involved will pay at some point when The Storm hits, but when that remains unknown to all but those within that inner circle of Q who have not yet revealed what they know or what to expect.

It all began in October 2017 when an anonymous poster on 4chan posted, leaving the signature of "Q" behind. They claim to have some form of security clearance in the US, which they refer to as "Q clearance." They post regularly in what is called "breadcrumbs" or "Q drops" in cryptic language with patterns, acronyms, and even timing deltas that must be observed to properly prove the validity of the poster in the first place. Often, these are filled with pro-Trump narrative, claiming that he will save the country as a whole. The most popular is by far, "WWG1WGA," standing for "Where we go one, we go all," a reference to a film called "White Squall."

Though the media is quick to paint it as a conspiracy theory with no followers, the truth is, there are thousands, maybe even hundreds of thousands, of people who believe this theory in which the government is filled with liars that are full of corruption. Up until recently, they gathered on mainstream social networking sites, such as Facebook, Reddit, and Twitter, but they have been systematically removed, one by one. Little by little, the Qanon movement has been quashed, attempting to silence it.

However, despite the attempts to eradicate it, the truth comes out—people are there, showing that they are, in fact, taking this in stride. They are ready to pursue knowledge at any cost. They know what to expect. They know that Q is there, posting for them, and they know that they can find the truth if they are willing to.

Common Resources

Now, if you want to do your own research about Qanon, you will have to do so strategically. If you use a mainstream search engine such as Google or Yahoo, you will find the information is suppressed. If you want to see what the truth is, you will need to use browsers that will not silence you. You will need to avoid the ones that are designed to try to suppress the information so you can see the truth. Currently, for example, if you tried to search for "8kun" on Google, you would be given page upon page of information about the site, usually from news outlets attempting to paint it in a negative light. However, using browsers that are not censored, such as DuckDuckGo.com, will allow you to search and find what you want without that immediate left-wing censorship.

If you want information from people who are discussing Q now, you would want to go to /qresearch/ a board hosted on 8kun. If you start there, you will find a list of the previous Q posts, notables, proofs, and more. Just about any information that you could want would be found there—but you would have to sift through it somehow. You would need to go through page upon page of other information, but you can find it there for you if that is what you prefer.

In terms of being able to find posts that Q has made without having to sift through everything, there is a myriad of sites that are designed to provide you with all of the posts linked up for you to see. The most common for a long while was qmap.pub, but as of recently, it had been taken down after people tracked down the IP address to a single person in New Jersey. It was one of the largest websites that promoted information from Qanon, allowing for aggregation of posts by Q. After the creator, Jason Gelinas, was outed on September 10, the site has been taken down. However, if it were to go up again, it could be a valuable asset in understanding and interpreting Q.

Now, Qmap.pub links to another site that can be used to track Q drops for you. Currently, the only site listed there for others is Q-resear.ch, a board that is known to have several Q posts included, while also tracking information about resignations, notable posts, indictments linked to the information that Q discusses, and a list of arrests as well.

There are others that come and go from time to time as well. A notable one is qposts.online, which hosts posts created by Q, links back to the original posts on 8kun, and also provides you with the ability to search for posts. This site is a great source for navigating through posts if you simply want to see what Q has been posted and find the original sources.

Ultimately, where you go for your own information is up to you, but you must be tactful about it. Use discernment. Do not be willing to accept something just because it was written a certain way. Do not allow others to take control or others to assert what they believe to be true if you cannot also fact check it yourself. You must be able to see the truth for what it is. Open your eyes. Become enlightened, and you will see what it was that Q had wanted you to see.

Common Qanon Themes

If you were to follow some of the Qanon posts and followers, it is first important for you to stop and consider the fact that there are certain themes that people use. You will run into certain themes over and over again, and these themes matter. The themes that you can expect to see will make understanding Q incredibly important. You will need to see that certain people come up repeatedly, as well as a certain feel to each of the posts that you get.

America First Patriotism

One of the most notable themes that can be spotted in the Qanon posts is that they are highly patriotic. The followers of Q are commonly referred to as "patriots," and they take this meaning literally. They will commonly go to great lengths to show their patriotism, with even the symbol for Q being regularly superimposed onto an American flag. Qanon support can be found all over the internet if you know where to look, and they regularly show up to Trump rallies with patriotic clothing on them as well. One thing is clear—Q asserts that he is closely working with the President and that they are together going to save the country. This patriotism focuses on this idea that the US must remain separate— that the idea of globalism would be a problem. The vast majority of the posts by Q will support the United States, attempting to back it and ensure that people will remain safe.

Naming the actors

You will also commonly see that Q will drop names in his posts—he will regularly not shy away from discussing who he thinks is a problem or who the Trump Administration is supposedly targeting. It is important to know that many times, the names get abbreviated.

You may see HRC for Hillary Clinton, for example. However, if Q is discussing someone, he will often leave enough there for you to tell who is being discussed so you can understand it.

Though at first, he was a bit vaguer with how he posted, with the intention being to maintain a degree of plausible deniability, it is also the case that these days, posts have become much more transparent. This is because of the fact that now, there are so many more followers that must be considered. The posts have become much more accessible. They are much easier to handle than they were before, and that is important. However, they are still usually veiled to some degree.

Asking for enlightenment

Finally, you will commonly see that Q recommends enlightenment—he wants people to open their eyes and see the truth once and for all. He frequently asks for people to open their eyes. He requests that people recognize that ultimately see that there is more than meets the eye and that it becomes imperative for people to understand this point. It is something that must be done: People need to see the truth, and if they do not, they cannot hope to achieve the enlightenment known as the Great Awakening that Q is attempting to trigger.

Chapter 2: The New World Order

"Hard to swallow.
Important to progress.
Who are the puppet masters?
House of Saud (6+++) - $4 Trillion+
Rothschild (6++) - $2 Trillion+
Soros (6+) - $1 Trillion+
Focus on above (3).
Public wealth disclosures – False.
Many governments of the world feed the 'Eye'.
Think slush funds (feeder).
Think war (feeder).
Think environmental pacts (feeder).
Triangle has (3) sides.
Eye of Providence.
Follow the bloodlines.
What is the keystone?
Does Satan exist?
Does the 'thought' of Satan exist?
Who worships Satan?
What is a cult?
Epstein island.
What is a temple?
What occurs in a temple?
Worship?
Why is the temple on top of a mountain?
How many levels might exist below?

What is the significance of the colors,
design and symbol above the dome?
Why is this relevant?
Who are the puppet masters?
Have the puppet masters traveled to
this island?
When? How often? Why?
"Vladimir Putin: The New World Order
Worships Satan"
Q"

This post, though difficult to understand
right off the bat, is straight from a post
from Q. November 11, 2017, Q had this
to say about. Let's break this down bit by
bit—in this post, Q asserts that there are
three puppet masters that exist in the
world. He lists out the House of Saud as
the wealthiest of the three, with the
Rothschild family as the second
wealthiest, and finally, George Soros as
the final puppet master. Soros is
commonly claimed to be one of the
founders of movements such as Black
Lives Matter and Antifa, as well as to the
Democratic party. It is often claimed
that Soros is commonly found where
nations fall and that, after living in
Hungary through WWII, he learned
about how to control the world—and he
does so through his own purchasing of

the media and misinformation campaigns. Now, we will be discussing him in more depth in future chapters. However, note that Q has listed him here as one of the puppet masters. He is someone to be wary of.

He also states that you must pay attention to the public wealth disclosures—the information on the statements is wrong; money is taken from place to place. It is moved around, and that many of the governments are feeding the "eye"—possibly referencing the puppet masters. Q asserts that these people are worshipping Satan—and references Epstein's island as a point of interest. This is imperative—it tells you that something is going on there—some sort of worship, and that we cannot know what is going on underneath it and that the puppet masters go there. He then names that the New World Order worships Satan.

What does this mean? It means that Q is stating that these people can all be tracked down. Q is stating that it is possible to bring it all back to a group of people worshipping Satan within Epstein's island.

Epstein, as we will discuss further, was indicted for charges of child sex trafficking. So, what does that imply was happening on his island, and what does it imply about the steady entourage of high-profile people visiting his island?

Within this chapter, we are going to delve into these ideas—we will scratch the surface and begin to figure out what is happening within this so-called "New World Order" that makes it as threatening as it is. It is important to understand that the New World Order stands for everything that Q is determined to prevent.

What Is the New World Order?

In Revelation 13:7-8, you can read the following passage: "*And authority was given it over every tribe and people and language and nation, and all who dwell on the earth will worship it, everyone whose name has not been written before the foundation of the world in the book of life of the Lamb who was slain.*"

This comes directly from the description predicting the Antichrist—which, according to Christianity, is the one who tries to substitute himself as Christ. He is supposed to be the downfall of religion, and he will be stopped by Jesus Christ's return to Earth. The idea of a one-world government, then, is one that precedes the idea of Q. It is not some theory that he has made up on his own— it is a prediction from the Bible itself. It states that the government gains this power overall throughout the world. It is the idea of this global powerhouse that is able to govern the people.

However, there is one thing that must be considered—the government can only govern the people in two ways—with the consent of the people authorizing the government to rule in favor of being protected by its breadth, or through the government dominating and taking control in a dictatorship, ruling out of fear. Either way, however, there is the involvement of the people, and even in a dictatorship, that dictator only has the power he or she does if the people allow it. This means that the real power comes from the people. Nevertheless, it is something that you must consider as well, especially since you have Q stating that this is something to be conscious about.

Q has, time and again, discussed the New World Order, commonly under the acronym of NWO. On November 12, 2017, the day after the previous mention of the New World Order, Q wrote:

"What if China, Russia, and others are coordinating w/PTOUS to eliminate the NWO?"

Now, this might seem dubious, especially given the current political climates between the three countries mentioned. However, that does not mean that it is an impossibility. It is actually quite possible that there are these further players that must be considered. It is possible that the Far Left wants to push, but most of the rest of the world tries to prevent it. Q thinks that this is possible, especially because he tends to contrast the idea of the New World Order with his own discussion of a brave new world.

"We are going to show you a new world. Those who are blind will soon

see the light. A beautiful, brave new world lies ahead."

"Your trust & faith in us is enough. You elected us to do the heavy lifting. Enjoy the show. BIRTH of a NEW NATION. NEW WORLD. Q"

He does not refer to it the same way as when he discusses this New World Order. However, it does make it clear that Q is trying to do something. Q wants to prevent whatever the New World Order is meant to be from coming to fruition. He is attempting to ensure that the government is fair and just—he wants to prevent the truth from being hidden, something that President Trump himself tends to assert as well.

Is It Real?

Is the idea of the New World Order real? It can be difficult to parse out. However, there is substantial reason to believe that it may be. Though you may not necessarily believe in religion and predictions, that does not mean that other people do not. Is it possible that the New World Order is trying to bring about the end times? Is it possible that they are trying to directly subvert everything with the sole intention being to take over the world and end it? Some people certainly think so.

There is plenty of reason to believe that there is some sort of New World Order lording over everything—think about how President Trump is painted in the media, for example. He is portrayed as being this horrible oaf that cannot do anything right. He is treated as if everything that he does is a problem and as if he cannot be trusted to do anything. He is treated as if he is the problem, and just about every mainstream media source will tell you not to trust him.

However, there are a few problems with this. First, consider what the mainstream media is. Who are the most common sources? If you were to go to get the news, where would you check first? If you have been in school for the last 20 years, you have probably been taught that you will go to the New York Times, the Washington Post, and the like to get reliable sources. However, they are incredibly biased—and they make no effort to hide it. This means that you will have to weigh your sources carefully. Know which sources are biased and which are not.

This is precisely what Q pushes—he discusses that the mainstream media is not safe. He discusses that the people are the media now—it is important to consider that the people are the ones that are able to get the truth out there. When you see that the media is not entirely unbiased, you can begin to recognize the truth, and that is precisely what Q wants you to do.

Chapter 3: Qanon and Donald Trump

Q posts about Donald Trump regularly, and likewise, there seems to be some degree of relationship between the posts made by Trump and by Q. This is imperative to understand—when you start to see it accordingly, you realize that there has to be some coordination between them.

When you are reading about Qanon theory, one question is asked regularly: How many coincidences are mathematically impossible? This is important to know—when you look at the way that many of the Q proofs that we will look at within this book, you will see several things that could be coincidental—but the truth is, there is no way that all of these different posts could be coincidental. It is next to impossible to have that many coincidences one after another, and you will start to see that as you continue to read.

In particular, Q and President Trump post at the same time on a regular basis.

This is commonly referred to as deltas—
a topic that we will delve into more in
the next few chapters. However, for
now, be aware of the fact that they exist.
A delta is the time difference between
posts. It would be, for example, if Q
posted something at 10:42:20, and
President Trump posted something
similar with a timestamp of 10:43:20.
This would have a delta of 1 minute. This
is important to keep in mind—when you
consider the deltas, you will start to
realize that they happen regularly.

Within this chapter, we will be taking a
look at these different ideas between Q
and President Trump, understanding
how close Q could be to him. We will be
entertaining the idea between the two—
we are looking at the connections
between them and figuring out if they
are actually related to each other
somehow. The connection between them
is undeniable—there is no way that they
could not be related to each other, even
if President Trump denies knowing
anything about the movement. The truth
is, there are so many coincidences that it
would be impossible for them not to be
connected. First, we will discuss what Q
has said about President Trump and

how he has posted that implies that he is someone that is close. Then, we will look at how Q has repeatedly encouraged Q and acknowledged the Q supporters that he has seen.

Is Q Close to Trump?

President Trump has been asked on more than one occasion about whether or not he is involved with Q, whether he supports Q, and whether he enjoys the influence of Q. In particular, on August 19, 2020, he was asked during a press conference what he thought of Q. His response was surprising to many people:

"They like me very much, which I appreciate. ... These are people who do not like what's going on in places like Portland and Chicago and other cities and states. I've heard these are people who love our country. I do not know anything about it other than they do supposedly like me, and also would like to see problems in these areas go away."

This appears to be an acceptance on his part, but that may not be the whole picture here. The truth is, President Trump is involved somehow—there is no way for him not to be. Regularly, Q will post something while linking to President Trump's Twitter account, usually to specific Tweets that were posted. For example, on September 8, 2020, Q posted a screenshot of a post from 8kun where he wrote:

*"YOU ARE WITNESSING THE GREATEST **[COORDINATED]** DISINFORMATION CAMPAIGN TO EVER BE LAUNCHED AGAINST THE AMERICAN PEOPLE. INFORMATION WARFARE. INFILTRATION V INVASION INSURGENCY. IRREGULAR WARFARE **[D]** EFFORTS TO REGAIN POWER. Q"*

Along with that screenshot, he included a link to a Tweet by President Trump that stated:

"The Democrats, together with the corrupt Fake News media, have launched a massive Disinformation Campaign the likes of which has never been seen before. They will say anything, like their recent lies about me and the Military, and hope that it sticks... But #MAGA gets it!"

In response to the Tweet and the screenshot, Q wrote,

"Digital soldiers #FightBack
Loyalists.
Patriots.
WWG1WGA!!!
Q"

What does this all mean? Well, for beginners, you see this support for President Trump. **"[D]"** is likely a reference to the Democrats in their efforts to destroy President Trump's reputation for the election of 2020. There are efforts to regain power in the sense that the Democrats are trying to take, or even steal, the election. It could be the case that the Democrats falsify the 2020 election to win back the Presidency.

Going back a bit to 2019, President Trump posted on May 17,

"My Campaign for President was conclusively spied on. Nothing like this has ever happened in American Politics. A really bad situation. TREASON means long jail sentences, and this was TREASON!"

In response, Q reposted the link to that Tweet, writing,

"*Be ready.*
Q"

What does this mean?

It means that Q absolutely supports or corroborates with what President Trump has stated—he is agreeing. He is telling those who committed treason to be ready for what will come next.

Additionally, there have been several times where images of President Trump have been doctored to be reminiscent of movie posters, along with several references to "Enjoy the show!" President Trump is always portrayed as a hero.

Another instance of Q posting in support of President Trump included him posting a link to a Fox News article titled "*AG William Barr Disappointed by Partisan Attacks Levied at President Trump Says Media on a Jihad against Hydroxychloroquine*" back on April 9, 2020. Along with this link, he posted:

*"Difficult to imagine media [D party]
attempting to squash all hope of a cure?
Difficult to imagine media [D party]
wanting the public to remain in fear [re
COVID-19] up until the election?
Difficult to imagine media [D party]
willing to sacrifice lives to regain
power?
ENEMY OF THE PEOPLE.
Difficult truths will soon see the light of
day.
Q"*

This right here asserts the idea that
media is not only under the control of
the Democratic Party but also that the
Democrats are attempting to subvert the
people to maintain power with ease.
They are doing their best to convince the
people to give over that power—to
ensure that they are the ones in control.
However, this is highly problematic for
all involved: What does this accomplish?
It accomplishes a loss of life. It destroys
economies.

One thing that Q has posted repeatedly
is that the COVID-19 crisis is not
entirely honest. Yes, there is a virus—but
according to Q, there is more to it than

that. Q asserts that the virus is being politicized and utilized. What could that imply? According to Q, it is an intentional attempt to destroy and subvert the US government and economy.

Trump's Encouragement of Qanon

Of course, despite claiming otherwise, Trump and his administration have encouraged Qanon theory and followers, whether intentionally or not. Most people are certain that it is intentional, citing that there is no way it couldn't be. There is no way that it could not be entirely intentional when you consider the way that he posts. There are lots of instances in which you can see that President Trump has posted his support and instances in which he has retweeted posts from people who are clearly related to Q or who are followers of Q.

One link between the two is the common repetition of the phrasing, "These people are sick." President Trump uses this phrasing in his own interviews when referring to the democrats and the DNC. Additionally, Q also uses the same phrasing as well. Q repeats this over and over throughout his posts, usually referring to the Democrats and the cabal that he was out to defeat. This is just one of the constant similarities between the two—it is imperative for this to be recognized. When the writing and speaking styles are the same between both Q and President Trump, you have to start to wonder if there is more to it than initially thought.

One example of President Trump praising Q, or at the very least acknowledging the Qanon movement, repeatedly retweeting messages about how he expresses his support for others and what he has done to do so. In what appears to be a reference or nod to Q, President Trump posted at one point a photo of himself, looking stern. In the picture, he is pointing directly at the camera and the picture is superimposed with the following text:

"IN REALITY THEY ARE NOT AFTER ME THEY ARE AFTER YOU. I'M JUST IN THE WAY"

This is quite similar to what you hear Q stating over and over—Qanon theory states that Trump is the one protecting the US. It is through Q's theories and posts that you see that they are connected-- Q touts Trump as the savior of the country—the last chance at the US to be able to successfully escape.

There have also been several Qanon supporters and believers that have been praised by President Trump. In particular, Trump praised Marjorie Taylor Greene, a Qanon believer who won the Republican congressional in Georgia, who is expected to win a House seat in November as well.

Trump himself seems to be well-versed in the theories as well, despite his proclaimed ignorance. For example, he has stated that the Democrats are snakes that are using COVID-19 as a political ploy, to using phrasing that is too on the nose to be coincidental, it becomes the case that President Trump would HAVE to be related to Q in some way, shape, or form.

Chapter 4: Key Players in Q's Game

There are several key players in Q's game that ought to be considered. These are people who are good, bad, and ugly. Some of them are on the right side—they are trying to overcome the corruption. Then there are those who are attempting to rule the world and those who are elite. These different people all have their own stakes in this story, and some of them may be deemed villains or heroes by the end. Some of these people's names may be recognizable to you from recent news, but one thing is for sure: Each of them has a role that they play.

We are going to take the time to go over several of these people so that you can better understand the context of what is happening. These are just a few of the key players that you will see throughout your time learning about Q. Some are the government. Others are shadow leaders. Others still serve to get people for the roles needed. Epstein, for example, has died in prison after being convicted of sexual abuse toward minors. Ghislaine Maxwell is currently being investigated as being one of the providers of children for corruption.

Q

We do not know definitively who Q is. We are not sure if he is a member of the Trump Administration, but current information points to the fact that he probably is. He would have to be to have access to as much information as he does and to have the degree of communication and coordination that he has had with President Trump. From hinting to posts that happen within seconds of Tweets Trump posts to posting images of Trump's office from obscure angles that do not reveal anything, there are all sorts of different ways that Q could have that access to Trump. Of course, we do not know for sure who he is.

He is the mastermind behind it all—he pulls strings, and he is communicating with everyone involved. He helps to figure out who is doing what. He helps to assert that he is someone that is intimately involved in it all. According to Dr. Jerome Corsi, the investigative reporter, Q is working to eliminate corruption in the government. Corsi discussed that the government had been trying to conduct a coup d'etat, but at the last minute reconsidered because Trump had agreed to run for the presidency in 2016. They agreed that if they got Trump into office that they could weed out the corruption naturally and legitimately, using the government to get the traitors out. QAnon, then, is the military intelligence that maintains that closeness to Trump. While Corsi never provided names or evidence toward this, it seems plausible to believe that QAnon and Trump are related, and it does appear that they are doing just that: Eliminating the corruption within the government in hopes of cleaning up.

Donald Trump

Donald Trump is the star of this show. He is the one in the role of protecting the people. He is the one who is supposed to save the world. According to some, he was specifically chosen to do the job. According to Corsi, he was approached in 2015 by a group of military generals stating that the US government had chosen Trump to run for the 2016 Presidency. According to Corsi, the point was to make sure that the Deep State officials were cleared out to prevent the need for an internal coup d'etat. Qanon, according to Corsi, then, is the same group of military officials attempting to remove and expose the corruption in the office.

This is further justified when you realize that President Trump has posted pictures of himself standing with 20 senior US military officials after a dinner. Shortly after the photo, Q wrote:

"Who is standing next to Pence & POTUS? Message? Bolton cleaning house. Out they go! A Clean House is very important. Q"

Standing next to Pence and Trump in this picture is Admiral Michael Rogers. He is the head of the NSA who, under the Obama administration, went to Trump Tower to inform Trump on November 17, 2016, that the Obama admin had been wiretapping his phone line, triggering him to relocate during his transition period to the White House.

Though Q is probably not Trump, Trump is believed to be the individual signing off on certain posts as Q+. This is because there was an instance in which someone known as VIPAnon received a photo after meeting up with President Trump that was signed with **(((+)))** after they had had a conversation about Qanon shortly prior. What is interesting, however, is that a key post from Q around that same time signed off with **(((Q+)))** instead of the usual *Q* that he ends his posts.

Though Q may not be Trump, Trump may be Q+.

The Bidens

The Bidens, as you will discover throughout this book, are believed to be highly corrupt. The entire family seems to be filled with corruption, from Hunter Biden being linked to Ukraine and receiving massive amounts of funding from them to Joe Biden's 2020 run for the presidency. However, one thing that you will regularly see throughout your time reading about Q is that the Bidens are highly corrupt. You will see that repeatedly, they are deemed to be highly corrupted and that they are going to have all sorts of issues over time. The Bidens are one of the last parties that you should want to see entering the White House, and because of that, there is good reason to understand that they are corrupt. We will be going over some of their corruption when we take a look at the later chapters.

George Soros

George Soros is one of those names that everyone knows but isn't quite sure why. He is a billionaire investor and major donor to many progressive and liberal politics. He is blamed for many things, from funding pedophilia rings and murdering off the opponents of the Clintons. He is someone who is usually blamed for just about every protest against nationalism that is seen. If there is a protest against the conservatives, it is probably due to Soros, according to many. Q asserts that Soros is more ensnared in all of this than you may think—Q believes that Soros is one of the big bankrollers, one of the puppetmasters of it all. Q believes that Soros is one of those big names that have the funding to control the world.

Soros has had a pattern of investing in countries and then destroying them from the inside out on more than one occasion. In the 1990s, for example, he traded so much of Malaysian currency that he was able to significantly devalued it. He has been ousted from several different countries. Six in particular—his organization has been banned from several different nations. In particular, the Philippines, Hungary, Russia, Turkey, Poland, and Pakistan have all banned his organizations stating that they cannot operate within the boundaries of their nations.

House of Saud

The House of Saud refers to the ruling royal family of Saudi Arabia. It is comprised of the descendants of Muhammad bin Saud, the founder of the Emirate of Diriyah, the first Saudi state. Together, they have ruled the country. The family is estimated to be built up of over 15,000 members, though the majority of the influence is within just 2000 members.

This group is recognized as one of the bankrollers in Q's posts. As we mentioned in the previous chapter, they are one of the groups with the highest degree of wealth of them all. They have plenty of funds, and they can use those funds to control just about everything and anything. They are recognized for their power and influence that they have over the world, and they are capable of pulling strings as much as possible.

The Rothschilds

Of the bankrollers of everything involving The Cult, the Rothschilds are the final that we will address. This family is a wealthy Jewish one, recognized as having a massive amount of wealth that has been amassed. During the 19th century, they possessed the largest wealth in the world. However, over time, they have been surpassed by even the House of Saud. The Rothschild family is consistently pointed toward as being the center of many conspiracy theories—but could there be a good reason for it?

The Rothschilds are another group that pulls strings behind the scenes. They remain in the shadows, not revealing the influence and control that they have. However, the truth is, they are everywhere. They control just about everything. Perhaps one of the most compelling points for this is that there are just three countries in the world that do not have a Central Bank that is run by the Rothschilds—these are Cuba, North Korea, and Iran. Even the US Federal Reserve is privately owned and controlled by the Rothschilds, Rockefellers, and Morgans. This means that the money that you use today is all controlled by them, and they make money off of making it. They are able to build and amass as much wealth as they have because they charge a premium to print that money. Think of this like them making interest—they are able to turn a profit on printing money because they sell the money for slightly more than it is worth. Perhaps that $10.00 bill that you just printed is actually worth $10.001, for example. However, that might not sound like very much, over time, that builds up. Think about it—if it takes $100 to get $0.01 back, that will add up rapidly. That is effectively a 1% interest rate. Now, imagine that you are talking about trillions of dollars. The GDP in the United States is estimated at $21.4 trillion for 2019. That is the amount of money generated by the US per year. Now, what if we took 1% from that? The answer is a whopping $214,000,000,000 per year. Now, that 1% is not necessarily the true value that is charged—the true value is hard to find at the moment. However, they use that very same principle to build their wealth up.

Additionally, the Rothschild family has been found to be linked to several wars that have come out. They have happened repeatedly throughout history, from about the time of the Napoleon Wars. Of course, there is not much about these shadow truths behind them all. They are working hard to figure out what it is that they can do to control the world. They openly state that there is no other advisor or company that will have the same degree of reach that they do. They know that they are unrivaled throughout the region, and they use it to their advantage. They are willing and able to leverage their name to take control of the world, bit by bit, making them a highly effective target to attack.

Hillary Clinton

Hillary Clinton is a target of attention when considering Qanon and the reach that it has. In particular, it is believed that Clinton and the Clinton administration are highly involved in the ring of people that are taking children and using them for adrenochrome—a byproduct of the body breaking down adrenaline. Clinton is linked to the theory of Pizzagate—a theory in which several Democratic officials were operating a trafficking ring out of a pizzeria known as Comet Ping Pong. According to this theory, Comet Ping Pong specialized in providing pizza as their front, but under the surface, they were also serving up children to use as people pleased.

Clinton became one of the people pointed at with all of these theories. In particular, you must consider the fact that if the Democratic party is trying to instate shadow presidencies, then there is probably a good reason for it and that any democratic candidate is probably also part of that overarching plan.

Clinton is regularly pointed at as being one of the biggest threats to Trump and justice. There have been trials about the emails found on her computer, and she is believed to be linked to all sorts of sinister projects. For example, consider the Clinton Foundation. They had a heavy presence in Haiti after the earthquake that decimated the region. Several children were lost, orphaned, or simply disappeared. Many children, all strangely with type O blood, disappeared from hospitals following the days after the earthquake.

This is relevant here—Type O blood is known to be the kind that allows for universal donating. They can donate blood to just about anyone, meaning that if the theory of adrenochrome is to be believed, they would be the perfect candidates.

Adrenochrome is believed to be used as a sort of drug-they are commonly found to be linked to these people. They commonly allow for the people to feel extremely high, and when studied in the 50s and 60s, it was found that adrenochrome created psychotic states that were known to be euphoric. To get that source of adrenochrome, however, people must be tortured while alive. In doing so, the adrenaline is able to oxidize to become the adrenochrome that the people are looking for.

Within just ten days after that first earthquake, 15 children had vanished from the hospitals—and these are just those who were reported missing. How many more were lost in the earthquakes? How many children were stolen?

If you are unconvinced, consider the emails that Clinton's advisor, John Podesta, contained. He regularly emailed using codes for both the pineal glands and adrenochrome. The pineal glands are responsible for creating adrenaline in the body.

In an email exchange, the following was said:

"I'm coming to town the week after next and will bring some walnuts!"

"Hey John, We know you are a true master of cuisine and we have appreciated that for years ... But walnut sauce for the pasta? Mary, plz tell us the straight story, was the sauce actually very tasty?"

"I should go through? I look forward to working with you (and maybe getting some of that pasta and walnut sauce dish!!)"

"We promised her a package, Rachel cleared that. I think we created one – like Walnut or something. Does this ring a bell?"

This is a reference to getting adrenaline and children. Pasta is a word that is regularly linked to children in these theories. Pizza and pasta were both used to allow for the discussion of boys and girls to state preference.

Jeffrey Epstein and Ghislaine Maxwell

Jeffrey Epstein was a billionaire financier who was charged with sex abuse of children. He was arrested on July 6, 2019, on charges of trafficking minors from 2002 to 2005 in both New York and Florida. More notably, however, is the fact that he owned a private island in the Caribbean named Little Saint James. His island was complete with a temple and several underground tunnels that went all over the island. Q asserts that the temple and tunnels were used by the cult during their performances of satanic abuse and cannibalism of children. His island was believed to be a common meeting ground, and the puppet masters, along with several other well-known and powerful people, have come out to this island several times.

One of those big names that went to his island regularly was Bill Clinton. He has been to the island at least dozens of times, riding upon the private jet known as the Lolita Express. If you did not know, Lolita is commonly used to refer to young girls that are overtly sexualized or used for sex, referencing the 1955 novel *Lolita*, in which a young girl nicknamed Lolita is abused by her stepfather. He became obsessed with young Dolores, nicknaming her Lolita as he took advantage of her. Nowadays, the word refers to "precociously seductive without connotations of victimization," meaning that the child is believed to enjoy it or was a willing participant in it all.

This means that in order to get onto Jeffrey Epstein's island, you had to ride the plane named after a child that was abused by an adult. Is this intentional? Quite probably—after all, how many coincidences can you really have before they are mathematically impossible?

Upon this island, the rituals were believed to be sacrifices for Moloch, the Canaanite god associated with child sacrifice. These rituals took place with boiling living children inside of a statue with a man's body and bull's head. The offerings are supposed to provide the people with wealth for sacrificing their children. The idea was that they could trade in their children, their most precious part of their life, for material wealth. It is a perversion of the typical relationship in which the children that someone has are the best things in their lives.

It is important to note, however, that shortly after being charged, on August 10, 2019, Epstein died in prison. His cause of death is listed as suicide, but the truth is that it is more likely to be murder than anything else in an attempt to silence him. This idea that he was killed intentionally is pushed even further when you consider where Ghislaine Maxwell comes in to everything.

Maxwell was a longtime partner of Epstein, who continued to engage socially with Epstein after their romantic relationship fizzled out. However, they were still quite closely related to each other. They spent ample time together regularly, with their lives closely intertwined.

An important factor to note is that shortly after Epstein's death, a reviewer on Amazon by the name of G. Maxwell posted a review for a book known as *The Book of Honor: The Secret Lives and Deaths of CIA Operatives*, written by Ted Gup. In her review, titled *"A comforting read after a personal tragedy,"* she wrote:

"A good friend of mine died recently under very tragic circumstances. Some of us saw it coming for quite a while, but it was still a huge shock when it finally happened. I picked up this book at the advice of a friend and absolutely couldn't put it down. I'd read it walking

*the dog, getting fast food, or even just
lounging around the house. It helped
me realized that my friend really
believed in something and that giving
your life for the CIA, NSA, FBI, Mossad,
or other intelligence agency is truly a
higher calling and not something to
mourn. A wholehearted
recommendation."*

If you are not yet convinced that this
was the very same Maxwell, consider
that on August 15, 2019, the very same
day of the interview, Ghislaine Maxwell
was found at In-N-Out burger reading a
book. What book may you ask? Simple—
The Book of Honor. Yes, that's right—
she was reading the book and
photographed doing so at a fast-food
restaurant the very same day as that
review. Coincidence?

In the recent past, Maxwell, too, has
been arrested for charges of sex
trafficking. She was arrested on July 2,
2020, on multiple charges of sex abuse
and trafficking in conjunction with
Epstein. Denied bail, she is still behind
bars awaiting trial in the summer of
2021. She was arrested in New
Hampshire in one of her homes after

several attempts to locate her. She fled but was quickly arrested. She has been formally charged with six counts, from transporting a minor for the purpose of criminal sexual activity (sex trafficking) to conspiring to entice minors to travel to engage in illegal sex acts.

The two of them were involved in grooming and abusing children together for their own personal pleasure. Even President Trump has made comments about how Epstein "likes them young," in reference to the women of his taste. However, remember that children are to women. Children are too young to consent and are too easily influenced and manipulated by those around them.

Chapter 5: Decoding Q

Q posts regularly online. He is often posting different things at varying frequencies. Sometimes, you will see just one word. Other times, you can have long posts that take up a few hundred words. Other time, all you see is a single image posted without anything else. No matter wat you see posted, you will want to understand what Q is saying somehow or another. Rest assured, it is not necessarily easy—it is not supposed to be. The reason for this is that if you have a simple, easy to decode method of communicating, you will not be commanding that same degree of challenge and information. People love challenges. They love seeing that they are understanding something and deciphering a puzzle, and when it comes to the posts that Q tends to leave behind, they are often complex.

Of course, if you have seen any of Q's posts, you would know that oftentimes, they appear to be strange. Sometimes, they can seem completely random or like they make no sense. However, each and every post is carefully crafted and intentional. Some of the posts are in prayers. Others call for everyone to remain together. Others are designed to create what are known as "deltas" with President Trump's own posts. Others are designed to hint at something happening in the future.

However, each and every post is there for a reason. While sometimes, the posts are listed out, it is important to recognize that there are also sometimes codes are written that must be deciphered, or there are patterns that have to be figured out. These can be difficult to track, but there are people out there who go out of their way to translate it all with ease. They go out of their way to ensure that people can understand them.

Understanding Q is often one of those things where people have to work to figure it out. It is difficult to do so, but it is something that can be done. Through practice, with a strong eye and a mind for patterns, you can begin to figure out what is intended. One of the biggest reasons people believe that Q posts on 8kun are because the people that are on there tend to have that attention to detail. They refer to themselves as "autists"—referring to their ability to parse out the details and figure out the patterns. Even the smallest of patterns are able to be deciphered by those with their keen eye for details found on 8kun. These people are willing to sit and work out the smallest of patterns until they can figure them out.

Within this chapter, we will be taking the time to figure out how to decode Q. We will do this in two ways—first, we will talk about deltas and their relevance. Then, we will look at the common phrases that you are likely to encounter in understanding Q posts and recognizing them. You will need to understand these different common phrases, so you know what it is that Q wants to communicate to you.

Understanding Deltas

Deltas refer to changes between variables in mathematics. It is the representation of the difference between them. Though Q is hardly a mathematical subject, he still makes use of deltas, encouraging people to look for the patterns and follow them along. In particular, you can see patterns of synchronicity between the posts that Q creates and Twitter posts by President Trump. The patterns are important to follow. The purpose of these deltas is to encourage the development of understanding the patterns that are present. When you follow the patterns, you can begin to tell what it was that Q wanted to get across. You will be able to tell that they were posting in tandem with each other.

On the one hand, you might assume that the connection is purely coincidental. For example, if Q is posting one thing right after President Trump has, could it not be the case that Q is just watching Twitter and posting as soon as he notices that Trump has? This is a fair point to mention—but the problem you run into is that President Trump is not always the first poster. Sometimes, Q will post a minute or two before Trump, and as a result, it becomes apparent that Q could not just be watching Trump. He would have to be coordinating with Trump. This means that there must be some degree of connection between the two to some degree, all backed up by deltas.

Now, of course, deltas of less than a minute are the most compelling. Sometimes, however, the delta is a year long. Other times, it is days, hours, or weeks. What does this mean for you? It means that there is some degree of coordination and speculation that must be taken beyond the idea of mere coincidence. For example, there have been instances in which Q will post a picture of a watch. That watch's time, when converted into a date, usually months in the future, then becomes relevant.

Tripcodes

Tripcodes are codes that are used online to generate anonymity while still maintaining some semblance of structure. On 4chan and 8kun, they create codes that act as a sort of pseudo-accounts that allow for you to be tracked and your messages to be credited to you without there being a need for any additional information. They are there to provide some sort of way of tracking so that messages will be followed. Otherwise, you could have one person post four different times supporting an opinion without anyone knowing about it. Imagine that someone posts an unpopular opinion—that opinion would be free to be reiterated by someone over and over with no tracking without a tripcode. However, with tripcodes, that is prevented.

Q has his own tripcodes that he uses, and that means that you will always know when Q does post something because he will always use that verified form of a message. This is relevant—without that, anyone could pretend to be Q just with a quick letter at the end of their messages.

On 8chan and 8kun, Q has changed his tripcode from time to time, always with transparency so that people will know about it. These tripcodes, however, have been referenced by President Trump as well, lending more credence to the idea that they must be connected in some way, shape, or form.

For example, on August 5, 2018, Q updated his new tripcode, confirming it to be *!A6yxsPKia*.

However, that very same day, shortly after Q had posted and verified his code,

President Trump had a strange tweet himself on his account. In his account, he tweeted:

"*Democrats want Open Borders, and they want to abolish ICE, the brave men, and women that are protecting our Country from some of the most vicious and dangerous people on earth! Sorry, we cannot let that happen!A so, change the rules in the Senate and approve STRONG Border Security!*"

Do you see it there? There is a very clear !A right in the middle of that post—it may be a typo, but could that really be a coincidence? How many coincidences are too many? Is this a reference to Q himself? Many believe that it is—and for a good reason. It is highly suspicious. It makes it clear that there has to be some sort of tie.

Common Phrases

When it comes to an understanding of whether Q is real or false, you will have to consider certain aspects of what is happening in his posts. You will need to be able to understand what it is that he is saying when he uses certain common themes and phrases.

The calm before the storm

This is a reference to a speech that President Trump made. In October 2017, President Trump was in a meeting with a group of military generals, and during the photography session, he stated, "You guys know what this represents? Maybe it is the calm before the storm. It could be calm. The calm before the storm. We have got the world's great military people in this room. I will tell you that. And we're going to have a great evening. Thank you all for coming." He was not willing to discuss beyond that at all. However, he also has made several different references to the calm before some sort of proverbial storm that he never really discusses in depth.

For example, just over three weeks later, Q posted, and as Q posted, President Trump wrote, "Very little reporting about the GREAT GDP numbers announced yesterday (3.0 despite the big hurricane hits). Best consecutive Q's in years!" Coincidence? Now, it is true that Twitter had a 140 character limit per tweet, but is it not interesting that he shortened quarter to Q in this manner?

And, when you consider the fact that a hurricane is a massive storm, you have to wonder if this is possibly a coincidence.

The same day, however, Trump also tweeted about how his administration was dedicated to providing the world with full disclosure and transparency to the people. He started it with the declassification of the JFK files, and just 30 minutes prior to that, Q was discussing the idea of transparency as well.

Since then, the calm before the storm became a common theme that you would see reiterated over and over again. The source of that storm, however, came from the movie *White Squall*, which involved people attempting to escape from a massive storm on a boat. In the trailer for the movie, which Q posted, you see several key phrases that Q uses on more than one occasion. One of those is "The calm before the storm." There are other notable quotes, including:

- Where we go one, we go all

- "I do not want to be who I was when I left—Anonymous."
- I will challenge them, and they will come together.

Each of these is relevant. They are phrases that are relevant to Q and how Q would post over time. They are also phrases that you will see if you were to go through Q's posts. The idea of everyone coming together is a major theme that is pushed—Q asserts that when necessary, the American people will rise together to protect and defend the nation.

Additionally, that reference to being anonymous is an interesting one as well. It hints at the idea of being on 4chan, posting anonymously. It is a reference to being able to be on the internet. Now, of course, we need to recognize the fact that the movie came out before the advent of 4chan and the derivatives, but it is a pretty interesting coincidence, isn't it? But, how many coincidences can there really be before they are no longer coincidences? Mathematicians know that it is statistically impossible for these to be sheer happenstance.

Interestingly enough, however, in June 28, 2018, Q linked to the trailer to White Squall. However, there are more coincidences than just that. The movie was written by Ridley Scott, and he was the founder of Scott Free Productions. Why is this relevant, you may ask? Simple: In December of 2018, President Trump tweeted:

"Michael Cohen asks judge for no Prison Time. You mean he can do all of the TERRIBLE, unrelated to Trump, things having to do with fraud, big loans, Taxis, etc., and not serve a long prison term? He makes up stories to get a GREAT & ALREADY reduced deal for himself and get... his wife and father-in-law (who has the money?) off Scott Free. He lied for this outcome and should, in my opinion, serve a full and complete sentence."

Notice the typo? What if it is not a typo at all and instead is meant to be a nod toward the company of Q in the first place? This is further iterated when Q, later that afternoon, posits the connection himself. Q wrote:

"The Art of Trolling the Fake News Media"

His guide included a link to the Wikipedia page for Scott Free Productions, along with his message of:

">>White Squall
>>WWG1WGA (from the movie)
Thank you for playing.
Q"

We are with you

Beyond the weather references, President Trump has repeatedly used the phrasing of "We are with you" every time he discusses something about storms. This is found when he tweets about hurricanes or other catastrophic damage that is encountered across the country. Q has begun to utilize this himself as well—he has on more than one occasion posted "we are with you" or WRWY as an acronym. Why?

Because Q is there for the American people, Q has asserted time and again that he is there to make our lives better. He is there to get us the transparency that we deserve and ensure that we are taken care of. He and the Trump administration are there to ensure that we are protected. It makes sense that Trump would say, "We are with you" in response to storms across the nation, but for Q to do it as well? It is a common link between the two.

The Great Awakening

The Great Awakening is a phrase that you may see thrown about often when looking through information about Q. The Great Awakening refers to the sort of enlightenment that Q is pushing for. Q is trying to get the world to see the truth—to recognize that ultimately, there is something wrong with the way that things are assumed. Q is there to try to convince people that really, everything that we know is built upon continuous attempts to deceive us into preventing us from knowing the truth at all costs. There are certain lines that we, as people, tend to take for granted or assume are correct, even without any reason to do so. These lies are important to dismantle and see straight through. If we are able to do that, we will also be able to do more as well. When we refer to the Great Awakening, we refer to the sudden realization by the people that what is happening is not okay. It is the sudden realization that everything that has occurred is something that ought to be changed. It has three key phases:

1. A degree of heightened awareness of the Deep State and what they are doing. This, of course, refers to the governmental entities that are currently operating under the guise of wanting what is best for the people despite being corrupt and attempting to expand and control more and more over time, even though the current laws may not work the way that they want them to.

2. Investigation of the Deep State and all known alliances. Remember, the Deep state is linked to several important factors within the US. They control the schools, the government from many different branches, the news, the religious leaders, and more. All of them exist to allow for a degree of control to be maintained and utilized. They are all lying to

maintain their own agendas without any pushback.

3. Recognition of what is happening and that those who currently rule the people are less interested in the people and more likely to assert that the general public is just collateral damage or even trying to harm us directly. They do not want people to know what is going on because when people know, people will resist. This is entirely against what they are trying to do—they are trying to tear us down, and they must be stopped.

Dark to Light

A common phrase seen repeated by Q and his followers is this idea of darkness into light. The fears that the true orchestrators have are that the people will learn to recognize the truth. As soon as their true colors are brought into the limelight, they lose everything. As soon as it becomes clear that the people are there to take control back and are no longer willing to put up with whatever nonsense these people are trying to push. The ignorance is the only way that the Deep State is able to maintain their subversion of the people, and as soon as that is gone, they lose it all.

This is what Q means when he discusses this common theme of moving from the darkness into the known light. He wants to expose the Deep State for what they have done once and for all so that the people can pass their own judgment.

These people are sick

Now, this is a phrase that you will also see echoed by the Trump administration. It is the idea that these great rulers have something that is fundamentally wrong with them. It is meant to refer to the depravity of the Deep State or the Cult. It is in part related to known and convicted sexual predator, Jeffrey Epstein, but it goes so much further beyond him.

The Cult, according to Q and the followers of Q, is a group of people willingly and readily engaging in ritual and blood sacrifices of children. In part, this is related to the harvesting of adrenochrome, a compound created by the body's attempt to break down adrenaline. This is just one of the important factors to consider. According to the theories that Qanon believers follow, the Cult is regularly trafficking children and torturing them to make sure that they are filled with that very same adrenochrome before taking their blood and killing them. The blood can then, according to these people, be utilized by people as a sort of drug, creating a euphoric high.

Q, in response, regularly refers to these people as "sick," and if you listen closely to the phrasing that even President Trump utilizes, you will hear it on more than one occasion. This is important: Both President Trump and Q are in agreement that the same group of people are sick or not right in the head.

Trust the plan

When Q talks, he commonly tells his followers to "trust the plan." This is important—the following plans are always a great way to guarantee that things will work out in favor of those who have created the plan in the first place. The Cult has its own plan, and we know that. However, what we must also trust is that Q and the Q team that is likely linked to President Trumps' own cabinet has its own plan that must be followed.

Remember, trust that those who are protecting you have a plan. This plan is one that is being followed closely, and it is designed to begin to tear apart the power that has been systematically developed by the Deep State. Did you know that the President today is far more powerful than he ever would have been before—and not due to Trump taking control himself? It is actually the case that these people have actually created a system in which the President has more power, and now that President Trump is the one with that power to utilize, the narrative has turned to show that President Trump has been trying to take control of more than he should have the right to do. However, this is not the case at all—the truth is that Trump is actually simply utilizing Obama-era loopholes that were created specifically for the Obama administration.

President Trump was not supposed to win the election—but now that he has, he is in an extremely powerful position, not even by his own doing. Trust that he will use all of the powers vested in him to protect the people. Trust that he is in a position where he is doing everything that he can to ensure that he is properly developing the success and wellbeing of the people. Trust the plan, and everything else will work out in return.

They want you divided

Another common phrasing to remember is that Q will repeatedly refer to the Cult as "they." Yes, it is an ominous phrasing—and for a good reason. In this instance, you will see that the Cult is attempting to divide you. Whether through racial tension, through pitting the different economic classes against each other, or even simply age groups, the Cult is attempting to push and encourage division. When we are broken down into small groups of people, whether by class, age, sex, race, or otherwise, we are less powerful. There is very real power in numbers, after all—just look at how ants, for example, are able to make the progress that they are. A single ant? Not very powerful—but when you bring them together, they can do great things compared to the general size that they maintain. They can build bridges or lift things many times their size, all of which is done thanks to their own cooperation with each other. Now, we are not quite the same as ants, but we can be just as powerful when left to our own devices and when we work together to provide ourselves what will help us the most.

The Cult fears this. They fear the idea that the people may come together to fend their whims off. They are terrified by the idea that they could be the ones who lose out. They fear the notion that ultimately, they could be the ones to lose out, and so they try to keep the people divided by any means necessary. They know that they can maintain their degree of power if they can keep tensions high between the people—and it is to their benefit to make it happen, so they do so by any means possible.

Q even hints at recent events, such as the death of George Floyd at the hands of police, to be false—intended solely to create the initial spark to light a fire between the people. They do this because they want to control—they want to maintain their semblance of power over those around them by any means possible, and they are willing to move heaven and earth to make it happen.

They think you are sheep

Likewise, with that fear comes a degree of conceitedness. The Cult, according to Q, will refer to the common people as sheep. This is a reference to how easily herded the people can be, or how easy it becomes to effectively control everything that the people think. Q writes that The Cult thinks that "you will follow the stars." This is a direct reference to celebrities or others in the media spotlight. The stars are those who the general public trusts—the people that are believed to be beloved and worth following or emulating. Of course, these people are not acting on their own. They are there to lead the people—people like you that may not know any better.

Q's posts, though becoming increasingly more direct over time, still tend to require some degree of understanding of critical thinking. This is because the whole purpose of Q's movement is to ensure that people are thinking critically. You must think critically to start to see the patterns that you will need to follow. Through critical thinking, you can start to see the truth, and you will see the corruption for what it really is.

Bigger than you can imagine. Expand your thinking

Something that Q repeatedly states is that something is "bigger than you can imagine." This is meant to serve to trigger followers to reevaluate what they see in front of them. It is important not to allow your thinking to be boxed in. You need to take a look at the world around you and what it has within it. You must be willing and able to understand that the powers that be do not like you. They do not want you to succeed. They want to take over and control everything. They have their hands in the banks. They do not want anything to be out of their control. But, until you are willing and able to stop and consider the wider picture, you will not be able to see the truth. You must go bigger. Expand your thinking. Let it grow into what it is supposed to be so you can see the truth in it all. If you can do this, you will start to understand what is lying behind everything.

Track the resignations

Q continually asserts that there are no coincidences—or rather, that there is o way that all of these patterns could be coincidental. This is imperative to consider—it means that when you see several people all resigning around the same time, there is probably something more to it. There is probably more to the idea that ultimately, there are people there hiding the truth. They may be retiring early, dying, being fired, or quitting. This is important—you can start to follow the connections and the corruption if you are capable of figuring out what you are doing. If you can see what you are doing, and if you can see how it all ties together, you start to see the patterns, and you can start to figure out how to track it all. All you have to do is make sure that you are well-informed and that you are willing to pay attention.

Their need for symbols will be their downfall

According to Q, the people in power who are trying to hide themselves become noticeable because of the fact that they need to follow their ritual patterns. Their need for their symbols becomes a way that you can see them. Their ritualistic symbols allow you to start seeing the connections. These symbols may seem to be innocuous, but when you realize just how many of them there are and how many high profile people have been seen with these various symbols, you may start to wonder what is going on. Stop and consider the truth—what is it that these people are doing? Why would all of these people have all of these symbols all over their bodies? Why would they think that this is the case? The truth is, you will be able to find out what is happening simply if you open your eyes and allow yourself to see the symbols.

There are several of them that Q has identified. Q and Qanon followers can expect to see symbols such as:

- Bandaged fingers
- Black left eyes
- One eye within a pyramid
- Owls

- Pyramids
- Red rings
- Red shoes
- The Y-shaped horns that are reminiscent of the goat deity Baphomet

But why? What is the purpose of these symbols? That is the million-dollar question here, and we do not quite have the answer. However, one thing is certain: People in power have been photographed with these patterns. Let's consider the blacked or bruised left eye for a moment. There have been several people photographed with this, including the former US President, George W. Bush, the Pope, Princes Andrew and Philip, and many actresses and actors as well, such as Robert Downey Jr.

Could it be a hazing ritual? Some sort of initiation into the group? We do not have an answer. However, in the past, black eyes were believed to be the 'devil's mark.' Coincidence? Possibly— but what have you learned through reading this book thus far? There are no coincidences when you have so many of them. It is strange that there would be so many politicians running around with black eyes on the left—either they are all incredibly clumsy, incredibly unlucky, or there is something more to it. There is a good chance that there is more to it than meets the eye—no pun intended.

Nothing can stop what is coming. Nothing. Now comes the pain

Q and followers commonly also state that there is no way to stop what will happen next. Justice will prevail one way or another. There is no way that it cannot. According to Q and those following Q, there is no potential way that all of this could be wrong or failed. This is simply something that must be done, and there is no way around it. The pain will come to the corrupt. They will discover that the world will not be kind to people like them. They will not allow for this change. According to Q, the day is coming when they will no longer be allowed to walk down the street. These people who have it all will see a complete and utter upheaval, and they will lose power. All you have to do is watch with your eyes open.

Chapter 6: Q's Drops

Q has had plenty of time to post various topics and considerations. Over the months and years, he has left thousands of posts. He has spent plenty of time trying to expose the darkness, and he does so with his drops, which are left at various times. He wrote on October 21, 2020,

"A deep dark world is being exposed. The truth won't be for everyone. Have faith in Humanity. Q"

Even in the recent past, he has focused on what he can do to provide the people with the truth and bring darkness to light, as he commonly writes. That truth is exposed, little by little, but it can only be shown if people believe what he has to say. He knows that he needs to do something to ensure that people recognize that he is worth listening to. He needs to make it clear that he is a genuine person, with genuine connections to the Trump administration. Those secrets that are being exposed may be shocking and disgusting. They may be hard to swallow, but the darkness runs deep, and the swamp must be drained for the betterment of everyone involved.

Also, on October 21, 2020, Q posted:

"Sometimes, you can't TELL the public the truth.
YOU MUST SHOW THEM.
ONLY THEN WILL PEOPLE FIND THE WILL TO CHANGE.
Crimes against children unite all humanity [cross party lines]?
Difficult truths.
Q"

What does this mean for the general public? It means that the general public is resistant. It means that Q knows that it is an uphill battle to get the general public to stop, open their eyes, and see the truth, and without them being willing to do so, there is no way to ensure that freedom can be maintained or guaranteed. It will take time. You will see people who resist or fight back against this idea that the world may be far more corrupt than they are willing or want to believe. As corruption comes to light, it will take time for the public to open their eyes, and they will need the

followers of Q to help them—to
recognize the truth.

There is a recurring pattern that what Q
says becomes true and that what Q
asserts will eventually be justified in one
way or another. His information is
sometimes predicted hours, months, or
even *years* into the future at times, and
that allows for this understanding—this
recognition of corruption and the
willingness to call it out.

Within this chapter, it is time to begin
delving into some of Q's posting history.
There is far too much to get into each
and every post, but we can go over
enough to make it clear that Q is on to
something. At some point, the
coincidences are no longer coincidental,
and when it gets to that point, it
becomes the case that you will have to
see this. At some point, you have to
acknowledge that the real problem is the
willingness to forego the truth to ignore
the patterns that are right before your
eyes.

Twitter's Policing of Posts

On September 29, 2018, Q wrote:

*"TWITTER has been given the green
light to blanket censor all content
deemed to threaten their SURVIVAL
[election]. GOOG-FB will follow.
EXPECT COMMS BLACKOUT
ATTEMPT (POTUS TWITTER)
[ROGUE_EMPLOYEE_EXCUSE]
Welcome to the POLICE STATE.
THEY KNOW IF THEY LOSE IT
ISOVER. THE TIME TO FIGHT!!!!!!!! IS
NOW.
GOOD V EVIL
HUMANITY IS AT STAKE
DROP THE MEMES
SILENT MAJORITY NO MORE
BE LOUD – YOU HAVE A VOICE
ARE YOU REGISTERED?
VOTE THEM ALL OUT
PREPARE
RED OCTOBER
WE STAND TOGETHER.
Q"*

This is a lot—it is Q stating that the
social media systems will begin to
censor everything. It states that even
President Trump's speech will be
infringed upon—that no one will be
spared and that no one will be free to
speak if it is going to threaten the
survival of the Democrats.

What is interesting, however, is that though Q posted this in September of 2018, the veracity of his statements is shocking. It is absolutely the case that media and social media have been drowning out the voices of the President and his cabinet. Just take a look at the news if President Trump says something that could even remotely be received as somewhat supportive of Q or appears to "incite violence," it is the case that once again, Q has predicted it. It took a while to really start putting the practices in place.

Between May of 2018 and October of 2020, President Trump has been censored on social media such as Facebook and Twitter 65 times while Joe Biden has been completely unchecked. What does this mean? It means that Biden is not on their radar—that they are not attempting to correct or police what Biden has to say for their own reasons. They have their own ulterior motive for this—obviously, the Dems want to ensure their victory.

Think about the perspective of the people that are cultivated when you start censoring an individual, slapping on inflammatory labels, such as *"This Tweet violated the Twitter Rules about glorifying violence. However, Twitter has determined that it may be in the public's interest in the Tweet to remain accessible."*

Think about it—this would appear horrible for the President—how do you justify glorifying violence? Many people, upon seeing that President Trump has had posts removed for reasons such as the above on not one or two, but *sixty-five times,* would be highly suspicious. It will even look like he is not a good candidate for the presidency if this is what he continues to do at each and every opportunity. How can he trust to run a country if he is constantly inciting violence?

The truth is significantly different than it may appear if you look at it from the other side. However, one of the first posts to get marked with this label was shortly after the rioting for George Floyd began. In his post that got flagged, President Trump wrote:

"I can't stand back & watch this happen to a great American City, Minneapolis. A total lack of leadership. Either the very weak Radical Left Mayor, Jacob Frey, get his act together and bring the City under control, or I will send in the National Guard & get the job done right..... ....These THUGS are dishonoring the memory of George Floyd, and I won't let that happen. Just spoke to Governor Tim Walz and told him that the Military is with him all the way. Any difficulty, and we will assume control but, when the looting starts, the shooting starts. Thank you!"

What is being said here? He is not threatening bodily harm to people who are simply minding their own business. He is not threatening the peaceful protestors. He stated that he would lay down the law if the governor of Minnesota did not get control of the rioting. He stated that he would send the National Guard, whose sole job is to defend the security of the nation, to shut down the rioting by any means necessary. Is this glorifying violence? While what was said probably could have been iterated without the same degree of almost excitement to the idea of violence, the truth is, President Trump is trying to defend his nation. He was trying to protect the city from being demolished for no reason. He is trying to ensure that ultimately, there are ways to protect the people and ensure that the nation was not torn down over rioting for a criminal.

This was neither the first nor the last time that President Trump found himself on the receiving end of being censored, but it is highly important to consider—it shows the truth here—that he cannot win. It shows that no matter what he does, there will be the media right there, painting him in a bad light. What does this mean for him and his presidency? It means that he will have his work cut out for him to ensure that he is able to speak freely to the nation that he has been chosen to run.

The only hope for the country, according to these sources, is voting. We must vote out the cancerous ideas, supporters, and the like. We must ensure that we do something to protect the status of this great nation one way or another. We have no choice but to move to ensure that we are protected, and ultimately, it all begins with getting out there and using our own voices. When even the President's voice is silenced, it is time for us to raise our own, to use our voices to speak out.

Tippy Top Condition

On 4chan on January 29, 2018, an anonymous poster requested something of Q. IN a message, he wrote, stating, "Maybe Q can work the phrase "tip-top" into the SOTU [State of the Union] as a shout out to the board?"

Now, the State of the Union speech was already solidified—it had been written and prepared in advance due to it being the next day, and those words never made it into his speech. However, Q and President Trump did deliver not too much longer—during the Easter address to the United States from the White House, President Trump had something to tell the world—and what he had to say may surprise you:

"Also, I want to thank the White House Historical Association and all of the people that work so hard with Melania, with everybody, to keep this incredible house or building, or whatever you

want to call it — because there really is no name for it; it is special — and we keep it in tip-top shape. We call it sometimes tippy-top shape. And it is a great, great place."

And what did Q have to say about it?

"It was requested. Did you listen today? Q"

Was this important? Was this really a reference that was meant to nod to a board of anonymous posters on the internet? Is it really the case that President Trump is trolling some of the most heinous, infamous boards on the clean net? Well, many Q followers believe that is exactly the case for this reason. Why else would President Trump have discussed "tip-top" in a speech to the people? Why would Q have drawn attention to it? Clearly, Q saw the request for President Trump back in January, and it did not go forgotten or passed up. Q saw it and knew that it was necessary, and somehow, influenced President Trump to use the phrase, not just once, but twice.

That's right. President Trump used the

phrase twice to tell the people what he was doing and what the intent was. This matters. This shows just how serious he was about what he was doing and saying. It also lends credence to this idea that Trump and Q are related to some degree. They will have to be if they continue to use these similar phrases at the same time. Otherwise, why would they be posting the way that they do? Why would they think that these connections would be ignored?

COVID-19—A Political Hoax?

Though COVID-19 is ripping across the nation, Q followers do not believe that it is a big enough deal to be concerned about. Q followers believe that the entire thing is highly politicized and, therefore, not really important to protect against. There has been a lot of backlashes, especially toward China, for the spread of the virus, and President Trump regularly mentions that the virus is a "Chinese virus" and that it is an invisible enemy that must be defeated.

Current beliefs have people questioning whether this virus is something that must be addressed. It is case that many people believe that COVID-19 is something that is being used as a tool by the Democrats. Whether released intentionally by China or not, the disease is something that must be managed and mitigated. On July 30, 2020, Q left the following drop for people:

"[infiltration]
Only those who could[can] be controlled [via blackmail or like-beliefs] were installed in critical leadership positions across all political and non-political Control and Command Positions [CCP].
CCP [necessary] to ensure protective blanket [insurance].
Traitors everywhere.
[D] leadership in joint ops w/ China [CCP] in effort to regain power?
It was never about the virus.
Sequence of events.
Flynn 1st strike designed to 1. cripple 2. prevent exposure of illegal acts [Hussein WH CoC] through NAT SEC [intel] discovery 3. Install 'controlled' replacement [rogue1_McMaster].
McMaster removal of 'loyalist' intel community_NAT SEC

Install 'controlled' [rogue2_ Coats_DNI] prevent DECLAS [House-Senate blockade].
Pre_Install [rogue3-6] > referral(s) to POTUS re:
McMaster_ Coats_ Wray_Bolton_ +++
Install 'controlled' [rogue7_Bolton] Bolton removal of 'loyalists' intel community_NAT SEC
Intel community [NAT SEC_WH] essential to control [infiltration] to prevent DECLAS_public exposure of true events [illegal surv [R] candidates 1&2, House members 1-x , Senate members 1-x , Journalists 1-x , Amb 1-x] + CLAS 1-99 events.
Mueller installed [Comey termination_loss of power][POTUS inside of a box][prevent counter-attack].
Impeachment installed [Mueller termination _loss of power][POTUS inside of box][prevent counter-attack].
C19 insurance plan _above fail
C19 installed [Impeachment termination _loss of power][POTUS inside of box][prevent counter-attack].
C19 _stage 1: Inform POTUS [intel + CDC + WHO + S_advisor(s)] _nothing to fear _do not close travel _do nothing [the political 'set up']

C19 _stage 2: Inform POTUS of Dooms Day 'inaccurate' scenarios [models] predicting death count 1mm+ [the political 'force'] _lock down [wipe economic and unemployment gains]

C19 _stage 3: Activate 'controlled' [D] GOVS to 'spike' death count + project statewide fear by presenting 'alarming' on-ground conditions [hospital [care-supplies] projections].

C19 _stage 4: Push testing, testing, testing to spike 'infected' rate incline due to daily testing inc [the political 'set up'] _controlled MSDNC failure to report death count [rates] proportional to 'infected' rate _deliberate miscounting of infected numbers [%] _change non_positive to positive _label death of non_C19 as C19 _etc.

C19 _stage 5: Eliminate / censor any opposing views [anti-narrative] [Ready when needed] Activate 4-year BLM narrative 4x power [use as division + [2020] C19 infect rates to justify close-limit until Nov 3].

C19 calculated [D] political gain:

1.   Eliminate record economic gains

2.   Eliminate record unemployment gains

3.   Shelter Biden from public appearances _limit public exposure of mental condition
4.   Shelter Biden from Ukraine exposure _narrative change _media focus C19
5.   Shelter Biden from P_debates [requested demands due to C19]
6.   Delay [D] convention _strategic take-over of nominee post conf
7.   Eliminate_delay POTUS rallies _term energy
8.   Eliminate ability for people to gather _ divide
9.   Eliminate ability to find peace – strength in time of need [strict Church closures]
10.   Promote mail-in-voting as only 'safe' method _bypass NSA election security [installed midterms +1].
11.   Push state-bailout stimulus [CA][NY] + wish list items
12.   Increase national debt [place China into controlling debt position _regain leverage]
13.   Test conditional limits of public acceptance [obey]
14.   Test conditional limits of public non_acceptance
15.   Test conditional limits of State authority [Gov-mayor]

16.   Test conditional limits of Media
[social] censorship
Who benefits the most?
[D]?
China [CCP]?
Russia is the enemy.
China is our friend.
[MSDNC [social media] programming]
All assets deployed.
Everything seen yesterday, today, and
tomorrow = calculated political
moves/events designed and launched
by [D] party in coordination with other
domestic and foreign entities in an
attempt to regain power over you.
Prevent accountability.
SHADOW PRESIDENCY [HUSSEIN]
SHADOW GOVERNMENT
INFORMATION WARFARE
INSURGENCY
Your voice and your vote matters.
Patriots stand united.
Welcome to the Revolution.
Q"

Long? Yes—but there is a lot to unpack here. Q gives information about several key concepts and thoughts. There is information about all sorts of different things here for you to begin to decipher.

Q refers to COVID-19 as C19 throughout the post and then asserts several claims.

One claim is that COVID-1 is meant to destroy the gains in the economy. This happens simply due to the fact that unemployment has skyrocketed. Thanks to the fact that the lockdowns across the nation, and even the world, have caused a significant amount of jobs to pause, and the current guidelines limit the activities of people, there are entire sectors of the job market that have been decimated. This is important to consider. By locking down the entire world, which Q asserts was done by those in power that do not want to be known, the economy was crippled, and sure enough, across the world, there have been significant problems for the economy, to the point that nations across the world have spent trillions of dollars attempting to stimulate the economy. That money comes from somewhere—and that money will have consequences.

Additionally, Q asserts that Biden is being sheltered, hidden away from people due to the desire to stay safe from COVID-19. However, this appears to be little more than an excuse that is being milked to ensure that his declining mental fortitude is not discovered. Biden rarely appears officially in public when you consider that he is currently running for President and when he does, he either appears to be not quite all there or like he is simply a puppet that is being used. Many of his answers are scripted and read off of a telecaster and that allows him to continue speaking, but it is also the case that Q and those following him believe that Biden is little more than the current mouthpiece of the Democrats and that he will not remain in power for very long.

There is more to this post as well. It states that long-term strategies for rallies will be slowed down or prevented due to the fact that gathering is not allowed. It is interesting that the Democrats have called for people to be allowed to riot in the streets to express their opinions and are called peaceful protestors, but the people who want to attend a rally for their presidential nominee favorite cannot. They are told that they cannot gather without serious restrictions. The numbers of how many can gather are dramatically slashed and prevented. The end result is people that cannot gather peacefully for their own personal or political purposes, but in cities like Portland, there have been recording numbers of protests over the last several months. From May 2020 to the end of October, there have been daily protests, and there is no sign of them stopping. They are ongoing protests against violence and police brutality, but the truth is, someone is funding it. You cannot just have five months of protesting without some degree of organization. The protests have led to at least two deaths and at least a thousand people being arrested.

Coincidence? Or is this part of the greater ploy? How is it safe to go out and riot, something that is going to cause an increase in heart rate and blood pressure, but it is not safe to also go to a pep rally where everyone is sitting and listening to the President of the country speaks? Rioting is violent—it is full of people getting hurt. Blood is shed. People scream. And yet, it is somehow deemed to be safer than the other options for gathering? COVID-19 cannot only be contagious and dangerous in certain settings. It does not mean to cherry-pick when it is contagious and only target people wearing MAGA hats. It is much less discriminatory than that—it targets everyone equally. So, it either becomes the case that the virus is not a big deal at all and is being politicized, which is why the Democrats do not care about the rioting. However, it could also be the case that the Democrats are looking to allow for the virus to spread more in order to allow for more lockdowns going into the election. This could cause issues with the election in all sorts of ways—can you have long lines of people voting if there are restrictions on gathering? This forces the need to allow people to vote through the mail—which is not nearly as secure as it would be if you were to go into a voting booth and vote on a machine. Ballots can be lost in the mail. They can be thrown away. They can be altered. Additionally, people who are not eligible to vote may be able to get votes in other ways instead. Especially when you hear the Democrats complaining that President Trump will steal the presidency or will lie and cheat his way to remain incumbent, you have to wonder if this is intentional. They are projecting—they claim that it is all the fault of those voting for President Trump while simultaneously using these very same methods to try to obscure what they are doing and prevent others from discovering the truth.

The Corruption of the Bidens

Joe Biden is currently running for President, but it is also the case that he is incredibly corrupt. He and his entire family are among several that need to be drained from the swamp, and especially currently with the election in 2020 impeding, it is the case that the entire Biden family has been getting plenty of attention, mainstream and otherwise.

In particular, Q has had a lot to say about the corruption that has come out about the Bidens. In more recent time, he has written:

"How do you inform your target(s) ['business partners'] what you have?
Why would H. Biden have such material on his laptop?
How was the content *originally* received?
Email?

*Why would H. Biden risk turn over such
material to a computer repair shop?
[contents unrestricted?]
On purpose [years of being treated
poorly by 'Pop'] or simple negligence?
If such information existed on a laptop,
why wouldn't contents be claimed?
Several attempts made to contact to
claim?
Messages left?
Why wouldn't H. Biden want to reclaim
knowing the contents on the drive
could bury *Pops* & family.
A troubled life?
A troubled family?
Looks can be deceiving.
Q"*

The context here is that Hunter Biden,
one of four of Joe Biden's children, has
recently been accused of having
concerning the material on his laptop,
which he sent to a computer shop to get
repaired. Within his laptops that he
wanted to be repaired, there were
allegedly emails detailing the
international business deals that he has
been accused of on more than one
occasion. Beyond that, however, it is
important to note that Joshua Wilson,
one of the top child pornography

investigators, has also subpoenaed the hard drive. It is believed that there had to be a good reason for this—why else would he be interested in a laptop?

There has been a lot of scrutiny of the Bidens, and in particular, of Hunter Biden. This is for all sorts of reasons— Hunter Biden had been discharged from the military due to drug use. He has also been seen in photographs with crack pipes and passed out. Currently, the suspicion is that he may have incriminating photos on his computers related potentially to his niece, Natalie Biden, who will be mentioned again shortly.

In another post by Q from July of 2019 that he recently reposted, Q has written:

"Example:
Joe Biden (Vice President of the United States)
>Follow the Family
Corruption in DC > How to Get Rich
Are Liberals willfully blind or ... ... ?
https://www.washingtonexaminer.co
m/15b-contract-in-iraq-for-bidens-
little-brother-exposes -obama-ahead-
of-debate

Biden's brother $1.5b contract in Iraq.
https://nypost.com/2019/05/11/the-
troubling-reason-why-biden-is-so-soft-
on-china/
Biden's son $1.5b deal w/ China.
Coincidence?
DRAIN THE SWAMP.
Q"

This was reposted on October 21, 2020, followed shortly by another post in which he wrote:

"You didn't think we highlighted 'Epstein' for no reason, did you?
Those who were once protected are no longer.
Timing is EVERYTHING.
Hunters become PREY.
Q"

This is important to note—especially with the name of Joe Biden's son being Hunter. It is implied in these posts that there is a severe degree of corruption occurring that will have to be overturned at some point. All of this corruption has to be released at some point, and there has to come to a point at which you can see the patterns. At what point are these no longer coincidences? That point is important to consider and matters greatly.

In another post from October 21, 2020, Q discusses photos of Joe Biden appearing to be inappropriate with a granddaughter. There are photos of the presidential candidate kissing one of his granddaughters on the lips on more than one occasion. This granddaughter? It is Natalie Biden, the daughter of his late son, Beau Biden. With a link to a NY Post article that depicts Biden kissing his granddaughter, Q writes:

"Inappropriate [sick] to you?
Normal to them?
Dark secrets.
Q"

This is important—clearly, the act of kissing his granddaughter is so normalized to him that he has no problems doing so out and about or where cameras will catch him. There are no problems with him doing so where he will have his photo taken. Joe Biden is *sick*.

There are photos of him sniffing the hair of underage children and women, making them uncomfortable. He has told stories about himself with other people that are strange enough to raise eyebrows and turn heads. One such story is one that he cited while traveling on tour in 2012. In this video, Biden can be watched stating:

"By the way, you know, I sit on the stand, and it would get hot. I got a lot of — I got hairy legs that turn blonde in the sun. And the kids used to come up and reach in the pool and rub my leg down, so it was straight, and then watch the hair come back up again and look at it. So I learned about roaches. I learned about kids jumping on my lap, and I love kids jumping on my lap." Strange? Many certainly think so. It caused quite a stir at his campaign at the time and has been reposted online repeatedly. With that, along with his repeated hands-on attitude toward women and sniffing women and children, it is easy to start becoming quite concerned about this man.

Firetruck Q74

Q posted on May 10th, 2018:

*"Fellow Patriots: What you are about to learn should not only scare you but intensify your resolve to take back control **(Freedom)**. The information that will become public will further demonstrate the criminal & corrupt **[pure evil]** abuse of power that the Hussein administration undertook in joint efforts w/ domestic and foreign dignitaries. The snowball has begun rolling – there is no stopping it now. D5. Stay the course and trust the plan. Protective measures are in place. Remain BRAVE. We knew this day would come. United We Stand (WW). WWG1WGA. We FIGHT. Conspiracy no more. Q"*

What is the relevance of this, you might wonder?

The context behind this post is that the President had negotiated for the return of hostages that had been kept in North Korea. On May 10, 2018, those hostages were being returned to the United States, and the President was there to greet them. In the scene behind them, as they arrived back on US soil, there were two firetrucks that were positioned so that they could hold a giant American flag. One of those firetrucks drew attention, however—it was labeled with the tag: Q74.

Strange? Well, it gets stranger. Q had recently updated his tripcode, and posts began to count up based upon the new code created. Somehow, the posts that he made went from single digits to be in the 60s, and over the next few days, they built up further. The post listed above was the 74th post on Q's new tripcode.

Post number 75 read:

"Castle LOCK Q"

This post came with it a photograph of an American Flag with the file's name being listed as "Freedom.png"

Just a few days later, on May 14th, 2018, Q posted again. This time, he wrote:

*"Image search for 'fire truck/ engine.' Is letter common in front of #? Post 74 Coincidence? U.S. Flag **[post]** 'Castle LOCK' – pointed ref? Comms understood? Q"*

This was an intentional nod to the post and the firetruck to get people to notice it. Now, the truck itself did not need to be changed or doctored—the station at the air force base where everything happened was already marked with 74 as their code. And, the truck that was used was a quint fire truck, referencing the number of pumps that it had. The truck would have been labeled Q74 prior to the post ever being made. Of course, there was no way that it would have happened coincidentally in that manner. The fact that the tripcode count jumped so quickly to allow for this to happen implies that it was entirely intentional. It was too perfect to not be.

"Honk for Q"

Though not initially started or posted by Q, this was a supposed coincidence that cannot be ignored. In Kansas City, Missouri, two people decided to take matters into their own hands. Curious about who Q was and determined to prove that Q was involved with the Trump administration, these two women made signs stating, "Honk for Q MAGA." They knew that on July 24, 2018, President Trump would be traveling through their area to speak at a veteran's convention. Knowing that they chose to stand on the side of I-29, where they knew that the motorcade would go. They tweeted a picture of their sign to the potus_schedule account—a Twitter account that is no longer active but appeared to be legitimate when it was used. They also Tweeted it to President Trump's own Twitter page, hoping that they would be seen. They posted pictures of the sign along with a message stating where they would be so that the motorcade would know to look for them.

A video was taken of the incident. As the women stood with their signs on the side of the freeway, the motorcade began to drive by. It was filled up with cars that passed without incident. But, toward the end, one of the SUVs honks. The honk is significant. However—the honk happened four times in quick bursts, and people quickly worked out that, in Morse code, the driver had tapped out the sound for "Q."

That's not all— Q also posted, linking to the video that had been posted on the subreddit, r/thegreatawakening, stating:

"We saw you! God bless Patriots! Q"

Now, you might try to state that someone was just messing with them or that they were just trying to stir up trouble. But, there is an interesting question that was posed by Q just a week later:

"How often does the Presidential motorcade honk upon request?" This was posted along with hashtags: #TryHarderMSM #AskTheQ

Coincidental? Maybe—but it feels too perfect to be coincidental. There has to be more to it than just that, and it is up to the people to figure out how.

The Veteran's Convention and Sea to Shining Sea

That same convention that the motorcade had been traveling to held its own references to Q. This drop also references other ideas. In particular, Q wrote, just prior to President Trump walking onto the stage, *"From Sea to Shining Sea."* Strange? Perhaps—but he had a reason for it.

As President Trump walked out onto the stage to the song, *God Bless the U.S.A.,* he gestured at the line "Across the plains of Texas, from sea to shining sea." With just five minutes separating these instances out, it appears that they had to be coordinated. There was very little chance that Trump happened to be on social media in time to see Q's post right before it happened. He acknowledged the very line that Q had referenced. Q had to know that President Trump was going to do so.

Additionally, the veteran that had spoken alongside Trump had a suspicious name as well. His name was "Alan Q. Jones," he stated during one line. That middle initial seems strange—how many names are there really out there that start with the letter   Q and are in common usage, and were in common usage back when these veterans would have been named? The answer is very little. The chances of a Q name are exceedingly slim, especially with everything else and the context that goes into it all.

Chapter 7: ObamaGate, the Shadow Presidency, and Draining the Swamp

The phrase "Drain the Swamp" is one that has existed for ages. It is a phrase that has been utilized since the 1980s in American politics. It is meant to allude to the physical draining of swamps to combat malaria by keeping mosquito populations down. That, in addition to the fact that Washington, D.C., was supposedly founded on a swamp, has been used regularly.

However, none has been as dedicated to this idea of swamp draining as President Trump himself. He has described his plans to repair problems and combat corruption in the White House as he is draining the swamp. Over the course of three weeks prior to his election, he had used the phrase "Drain the swamp" a whopping 79 times. That is nearly four times per day.

Clearly, this is a major point of focus for the president. He cares about doing so and is pushing the idea as much as possible. He has even gone as far as to refer to certain people that he believes are unscrupulous as "swamp monsters," and many others have adopted this sort of language.

For President Trump, he pushes certain ideas at the rallies. Build the wall. Lock her up. Drain the swamp. These are all short, sweet phrases to push the ideas that he cares to address. These ideas are meant to be motivating, captivating, and help him to secure his reelection. He makes notes of his plans—he intends to clear the swamp and make sure that the government is made honest again. He promises to drain the swamp and get rid of the corruption that exists within the nation. But, can he do it?

It all comes back down to Obamagate. This is the idea that Obama's presidency was not legitimate. According to President Trump, his presidency ought to have been questioned and scrutinized further. This is commonly seen in Q's posts as well. There are so many of them questioning the legitimacy of President Obama and stating that he had no real claim.

Let's take a look at a post given by Q on
May 24, 2020:

"Relevance re: [Susan Rice] 'top secret'
[DECLAS] paragraph:

*"From a national security perspective,
Comey said he does have some concerns
that incoming NSA Flynn is frequently
speaking with Russian Ambassador
Kislyak. Comey said that could be an
issue as it relates to sharing sensitive
information. President Obama asked if
Comey was saying that the NSC should
not pass sensitive information related
to Russia to Flynn. Comey replied
'potentially.'"*

*What was really discussed during [Jan
5] meeting?*

*[Hussein] order preventing sharing of
intel re: Russia?*

*Would such an order shield [Hussein]
admin from discovery re: Obamagate?*

*Would such an order shield [Clinton]
camp from discovery re: Clinton-DNC
Russian collusion?*

Would such an order be known to
POTUS or CLASSIFIED?

If CLASSIFIED how could it be
discovered?

NSA Mike Rogers _ step down [retire]
[date]?

NSA Mike Rogers _ TT [SCIF secure]
[date]?

[Brennan][Clapper][Carter] push to
TERM _ NSA Mike Rogers [date]?

WASH POST:

"The heads of the Pentagon and the
nation's intelligence community have
recommended to President Obama that
the director of the National Security
Agency, Adm. Michael S. Rogers, be
removed. The recommendation,
delivered to the White House last
month, was made by Defense Secretary
Ashton B. Carter and Director of
National Intelligence James R. Clapper
Jr., according to several U.S. officials
familiar with the matter."

HOW DO YOU CIRCUMVENT THE SHADOW INTEL COMM?

https://theintercept.com/2017/12/04/trump-white-house-weighing-plans-for-private-spies-to-counter-deep-state-enemies/

Critical thinking _what did [Susan Rice] DECLAS [Jan 5] WH meeting reveal?

RUSSIA INTEL HOLD

HOW DO YOU ADD LAYERS OF PROTECTION?

INSTALL A SPECIAL COUNSEL TO LOCK [FREEZE] EVERYTHING RE: RUSSIA?

INSTRUCT AND COORD W: NSC [INTEL COMMUNITY] [SCHIFF ARMS LENGTH] TO INITIATE WHISTLEBLOWER ALLEGATIONS 1-9?

INSTRUCT CONGRESS TO FILE ARTICLES OF IMPEACHMENT?

COORD W: CHINA TO TERM ECON - UNEMPLOYMENT - GAINS, INITIATE LOCKDOWN DUE TO HEALTH CONCERNS, PUSH FEAR THROUGH DNC MEDIA, INSTRUCT GOVERNORS UNDER CONTROL TO ENACT VOTE-BY-MAIL?

COINCIDENCE JAN 15

1. IMPEACHMENT ARTICLES DELIVERED TO SENATE [HELD]

2. CHINA PHASE 1 USA CLAWBACK DEAL SIGNED

3. 1ST COVID-19 CASE LANDED SEATTLE

ALL ASSETS DEPLOYED.

WIN BY ANY MEANS NECESSARY.

EVERYTHING IS AT STAKE.

Welcome to the Shadow Presidency of Barack H. Obama.

Q"

Now, that is quite the post there—but you need to realize that it is actually that long for a reason. There is much to be deciphered here, and it is made to discuss the illegitimacy of Obama. It starts with noting that Flynn's discussions with the Russian Ambassador Kislyak would be deemed concerning to Comey. What does this mean? It means that some of the actions happening under the Obama administration probably should not have been happening.

Q asserts that much of what has happened is to defend against the fact that just about everything is at stake, and there certainly is a lot. The shadow presidency of Obama is referenced regularly by Q. He states regularly that Obama was the result of a shadow presidency and that he did not actually hold any power. Is this the case? Potentially—many people believe so.

Let's take some time to revisit another post that we looked at earlier::

"[infiltration]
Only those who could[can] be
controlled [via blackmail or like-beliefs]

were installed in critical leadership positions across all political and non-political Control and Command Positions [CCP].
CCP [necessary] to ensure protective blanket [insurance].
Traitors everywhere.
[D] leadership in joint ops w/ China [CCP] in effort to regain power?
It was never about the virus.
Sequence of events.
Flynn 1st strike designed to 1. cripple 2. prevent exposure of illegal acts [Hussein WH CoC] through NAT SEC [intel] discovery 3. Install 'controlled' replacement [rogue1_McMaster].
McMaster removal of 'loyalist' intel community_ NAT SEC
Install 'controlled' [rogue2_ Coats_DNI] prevent DECLAS [House-Senate blockade].
Pre_Install [rogue3-6] > referral(s) to POTUS re:
McMaster_ Coats_ Wray_ Bolton_ +++
Install 'controlled' [rogue7_Bolton]
Bolton removal of 'loyalists' intel community_ NAT SEC
Intel community [NAT SEC_WH] essential to control [infiltration] to prevent DECLAS_public exposure of true events [illegal surv [R] candidates

1&2, House members 1-x , Senate members 1-x , Journalists 1-x , Amb 1-x] + CLAS 1-99 events.

Mueller installed [Comey termination_loss of power][POTUS inside of a box][prevent counter-attack].

Impeachment installed [Mueller termination _loss of power][POTUS inside of box][prevent counter-attack].

C19 insurance plan _above fail

C19 installed [Impeachment termination _loss of power][POTUS inside of box][prevent counter-attack].

C19 _stage 1: Inform POTUS [intel + CDC + WHO + S_advisor(s)] _nothing to fear _do not close travel _do nothing [the political 'set up']

C19 _stage 2: Inform POTUS of Dooms Day 'inaccurate' scenarios [models] predicting death count 1mm+ [the political 'force'] _lock down [wipe economic and unemployment gains]

C19 _stage 3: Activate 'controlled' [D] GOVS to 'spike' death count + project statewide fear by presenting 'alarming' on-ground conditions [hospital [care-supplies] projections].

C19 _stage 4: Push testing, testing, testing to spike 'infected' rate incline due to daily testing inc [the political 'set

up'] _controlled MSDNC failure to report death count [rates] proportional to 'infected' rate _deliberate miscounting of infected numbers [%] _change non_positive to positive _label death of non_C19 as C19 _etc.
C19 _stage 5: Eliminate / censor any opposing views [anti-narrative] [Ready when needed] Activate 4-year BLM narrative 4x power [use as division + [2020] C19 infect rates to justify close-limit until Nov 3].
C19 calculated [D] political gain:
1. Eliminate record economic gains
2. Eliminate record unemployment gains
3. Shelter Biden from public appearances _limit public exposure of mental condition
4. Shelter Biden from Ukraine exposure _narrative change _media focus C19
5. Shelter Biden from P_debates [requested demands due to C19]
6. Delay [D] convention _strategic take-over of nominee post conf
7. Eliminate_delay POTUS rallies _term energy
8. Eliminate ability for people to gather _ divide

*9. Eliminate ability to find peace –
strength in time of need [strict Church
closures]*
*10. Promote mail-in-voting as only
'safe' method _bypass NSA election
security [installed midterms +1].*
*11. Push state-bailout stimulus
[CA][NY] + wish list items*
*12. Increase national debt [place China
into controlling debt position _regain
leverage]*
*13. Test conditional limits of public
acceptance [obey]*
*14. Test conditional limits of public
non_ acceptance*
*15. Test conditional limits of State
authority [Gov-mayor]*
*16. Test conditional limits of Media
[social] censorship*
Who benefits the most?
[D]?
China [CCP]?
Russia is the enemy.
China is our friend.
[MSDNC [social media] programming]
All assets deployed.
*Everything seen yesterday, today, and
tomorrow = calculated political
moves/events designed and launched
by [D] party in coordination with other*

domestic and foreign entities in an
attempt to regain power over you.
Prevent accountability.
SHADOW PRESIDENCY [HUSSEIN]
SHADOW GOVERNMENT
INFORMATION WARFARE
INSURGENCY
Your voice and your vote matters.
Patriots stand united.
Welcome to the Revolution.
Q"

This post is meant to remain hidden, of course—it is not meant to see the light of day. If you were to search for it online, you would have a hard time finding it. The pages that would have this information remain hidden or difficult to work out. It is the case that this information is meant to be hidden so that people do not find out the truth. Think about everything that was packed into that drop. That drop was meant to accuse the presidency of Obama as being illegitimate for a reason—it was meant to show you that the enemy is out there, trying to take control of everything that you do. He posts further:

"The point to understand.

They [knowingly] unmasked [attached names to] AFTER POTUS won the election of 2016.
They thought they could prevent the exposure of this information and remain protected.
Why did they believe this?
What 'insurance' did they have?
Infiltration of US GOV?
This fact alone should scare every American.
SHADOW PRESIDENCY.
SHADOW GOVERNMENT.
It took this long for a reason.
Q"

What does this mean and imply? It means that there is a point in which there needs to be a consideration of the shadow presidency. The government and presidency were illegitimate—they were fronts for something that was meant to be far more sinister—the corrupt Cult that has been referenced throughout this book. The cult was there, allowing them to remain hidden with information that should never have seen the light of day. They had the fact that they had insurance—some sort of way that they could prevent the exposure of everything, and that is a problem for the average person. You should be afraid—very afraid—of this fact.

Q has gone further to implicate several other people in this scheme. On May 9, 2020, he posted:

"THE SHADOW PRESIDENCY.
THE SHADOW GOVERNMENT.
Why did [Hussein] shadow POTUS re: [F] trips?
Why did [Kerry] shadow POTUS re: Iran?
Why did [Kerry] shadow POTUS re: [CLAS 1-99]?
Why did [McMaster] target and remove loyal intel operatives inside WH?
Why did [McMaster] prevent declas-disclose to Congress?
Why did [Coats] prevent declas-disclose to Congress?
Why did [Bolton] prevent decals-disclose to Congress?
Why did [Ryan] prevent subpoena power of (R) Congress?
Why did [Rosenstein] work to entrap and install blockade [SC]?
Why did [Rosenstein] install [Mueller] knowing zero evidence of Russia collusion?

*Why did [Mueller] attempt to retake
FBI DIR position?
Why did [Mueller][Rosenstein] drag out
SC investigation if known no Russia
collusion pre + start?
Why did select members of
[NSC][Vindman] actively leak to MSM?
Why did select members of
[NSC][Vindman] orchestrate fake
whistleblower report w/
[Schiff][Atkinson][CLAS 1-9] to
sabotage and initiate impeachment?
Why did [Pelosi] rush impeachment
investigation?
Why did [Pelosi] then hold
impeachment article(s) until Jan 15?
Why did [Schiff] push false 'Russia
evidence' narrative post closed door
interviews [no evidence of collusion]?
Why did [Schiff] coordinate w/ WH
NSC [through proxy] to arrange for
Ukraine whistleblower?
Why did [Schiff] actively leak
knowingly false statements during-post
classified sessions to MSM?
Why did [Schiff] illegally surveil
[phone] members of WH legal team,
media, and Congress?
What Pentagon officials [CLAS 1-99
_subject] tendered resignation within a
2 week period?*

Why did [Omarosa Manigault Newman] attempt to entrap POTUS through secret and illegal recordings? Why did [Soros] finance anti-POTUS events and organizations across US? Why did [CLAS 1-99] organize and push propaganda [smear] campaign through use of MSM & Hollywood?
[CLAS 1-99][F]
[CLAS 1-99][F]
[CLAS 1-99][F]
[CLAS 1-99][F]
[CLAS 1-99]
[CLAS 1-99]
[CLAS 1-99]
[CLAS 1-99]
[CLAS 1-99] x 49
INSURGENCY.
IRREGULAR WARFARE.
THE GREATEST POLITICAL SCANDAL IN HISTORY.
What are they trying to prevent?
Who are they trying to protect?
Q"

In this post, he calls out Barack Obama with the codename [Hussein] in order to reference Obama's middle name. In this post, Q mentions that several of the recent occurrences in the White House simply do not make sense—it does not make sense for people to choose to do these things in this way. When you take a look at the different actions, you can start to question it. Why would McMaster want to remove operatives if he weren't hiding something? And, why would he be working to prevent information from being disclosed? That is not something that you do if you are not hiding anything. Why would any of this happen?

The answer is simple: There was corruption. There were pushes of false narratives and crimes that never occurred to try to control the people and the government. This was all a last-ditch effort meant to try to somehow take control.

The end result here is simple—there is some degree of shadow presidency occurring that you will need to be able to navigate past. There is some degree of problem that will need to be overcome. This shadow presidency was little more than a farce to convince people that there was no problem in the first place.

When it comes to draining the swamp of this corruption and this shadow presidency, then, Q discusses the game's plan. On October 18, 2020, Q posted:

"HOW IS THE GAME PLAYED?

Example:

https://www.politico.com/news/2020/ 10/08/hunter-biden-business-partner-fraud-428154

1. Unanimous convicted by Jury

2. Overturn of conviction by Judge Ronnie Abrams of the Southern District of New York [attempt to free _provide 'shade' H. Biden?]

3. Federal Appeals Court reinstates conviction

Background Judge Ronnie Abrams?

https://www.courthousenews.com/jud ge-wed-mueller-team-member-steps-away-trump-suits/

Married to Greg Andres?

Who is Greg Andres?

https://fr.reuters.com/article/us-usa-trump-russia-lawyer-exclusive-idUSKBN1AH5F9

DRAIN THE SWAMP.

Q"

What this means is that there is a certain game being played right now to drain the swamp. Right now, we are right back to Hunter Biden—and in this instance, we are looking at how he is important. We are right back to look at how to drain the swamp for a good reason.

Hunter Biden was not implicated in a case that held his business partner responsible for fraud. He was protected by his lawyer, stating that his name, though invoked, was used without his knowledge and that Biden had stepped out as soon as he learned about the corruption. Did he really? It is hard to know one way or another.

The conviction was overturned by Judge Ronnie Abrams. However, this person is married to Greg Andres, a lawyer in New York specializing in foreign bribery and fraud, and he is part of a team of lawyers that were investigating the coordination between Russia and Trump. This connection might seem like no big deal, but think about it—you have someone who is working to overthrow President Trump married to the judge who exonerated the son of Trump's political opponent. This is interesting to note—and there are some notes that President Trump's team is working to combat the conflicts surrounding the issue.

This is precisely the kind of corruption that President Trump is looking to eliminate. By being capable of eliminating the issues at hand, the corruption that protects those who do not deserve protection is what happens. It is the case that this sort of corruption needs to be eliminated. It needs to be stopped to prevent corruption from continuing, but that requires a certain degree of understanding. It requires recognition that there are people in power that should not be, and that needs to be rejected to ensure that the people are protected. We deserve a nation that is founded upon justice, and when the entire government is corrupt, there is no justice to be found.

Chapter 8: The Presidential Elections

It is the case that Q and followers of Q are concerned that the 2020 presidential election will be rigged. There have already been attempts to subvert it—we've seen this in several different contexts, such as taking a look at what happened with COVID-19. As we have discussed, Q has implied that COVID-19 being as bad as it was intentional—it is to impede upon the elections. The election will be stretched out if votes are not officially counted by Election Day. It is the case that the election becomes easier to tamper with in this state.

Of course, the Left is already framing things with the context that things will be wrong if President Trump wins. You already see that the surveys show that Biden is almost definitely going to win—but you saw the same with Trump's loss predicted in 2019. The truth is, you need to look wider. They will not go down without a fight. Trump was not supposed to win the presidency in 2016, and yet he did—you can bet that they are trying to control the 2020 election to regain control as well.

What does this mean?

It means that the upcoming election will be disastrous.

According to Q, there have already been several attempts to tank the chances of President Trump being elected. As written on October 1, 2020:

"Spy campaign failed.
Russia Russia Russia failed.
Weissmann [Mueller] failed.
Leaks failed.
Fake news reports failed.
Impeachment failed.
CDC/WHO recommend 'do not close' border failed."

The very same post has gone on to question what would have happened if COVID19 had not been a concern? All of Biden's ammunition used during the debate would be gone. Voting would not be via mail-in ballots. There would be fewer options for fraud. There would be fewer options for getting Biden into office. The truth is, this is all one big ploy. This is one big game meant to get Trump out of office because the Powers that Be didn't want him there anyway. So what happens next? What happens when he refuses to step down or when he wins the next election?

Right before the 2020 election, it has become the case that there are several people who are being outed. The entire Biden family is currently under intense scrutiny. Biden himself has barely been able to contain himself in interviews and debates. The entire election is predicted to be one big disaster, and it is very little we can do at this point but trust that everything will work out and that the corruption will be discovered.

In September of 2020, Q wrote:

"Add it all up.
1. Virus
2. Riots [organized _ANTIFA]
3. Fires
The 'Why':
https://www.youtube.com/watch?v=c
UxilJznKyY
Make no mistake, they will not concede on Election Night.

Make no mistake, they will contest this legally in battleground states.
Make no mistake, they will project doubt in the election results
Make no mistake, they will organize massive riots and attempt Anarchy-99 design
Playbook known.
Q"

This is once again calling out the attempts to get the Democrats back into office. This is once again attempting to get everything back in favor of the Powers that Be that want their shadow president back. We've seen it all—every time that an attempt to get Trump out failed, something worse happened. It started with the virus and the lockdowns. Then, it was the death of George Floyd, something that many believe was already overblown. Then, it was the riots and fires that came after. They've tried it all. They're growing more desperate and they have no real recourse at this point. There is nothing that they can do that will help them. There is nothing else that they can do that will help them aside from lying and attempting to tear their way into the election illegitimately.

Keep your eyes open. Be ready to vote and do not be afraid to call out any corruption that you see. This is especially imperative when you consider the fraud going viral. In a video released on October 20, 2020 based in Germantown, Maryland, there is a video in which a man, counting ballots, stops, looks around, picks up a pen, and starts filling in a ballot. The camera shortly after pans away to prevent it from recording any more of the alteration of the ballot. Is this secure? Is this really a way that you can properly vote in an election without fraud?

The Trump administration has voiced repeatedly that they have doubts about the veracity of those mail-in ballots. They have doubted that they are able to be as controlled and regulated as they would need to be. Ballots have gone missing. They've turned up in strange places so that they would go uncounted. Some people have more than one. What does this do for the general people? It causes all sorts of issues.

The election, no matter what happens, will spark the beginning of a disaster. At this point, no matter who wins, there will be a backlash. There will be resistance. There will be people who refuse to accept the results and at this point, only time will tell what will happen.

Chapter 9: The Great Awakening: Q's End Goal of Enlightenment

At this point, you've read through much of the book. You've got a pretty solid understanding of what Q is and what his end goal is: Enlightenment. Q is trying to bring the world to a state of enlightenment in which everyone involved is able to think rationally and clearly. Now that you understand that Q is here to be a conduit of the truth and is here to provide that truth to everyone, that you will be able to recognize that he wants to benefit everyone. He is here to show everyone the truth—to reveal the lies and take the masks off from those who are lying and trying to take advantage of the general population. It is time for you to see the truth. It is time for you to become enlightened.

Enlightenment can be difficult. It can be hard to cope with this idea that truth is not what you thought it was. It can be difficult for you to really come to terms with what is happening around you. It can be hard for you to figure out what you are doing and how you can navigate it. When it comes to seeing the truth, you will see it all around you. President Trump is not the monster that the media is trying to portray him as. He is not this horrible beast of a man that is trying to tear apart the country. On the contrary—he is trying to clean it up. He is trying to protect the people, to ensure that the people are going to know what they are doing. He knows that the nation is full of corruption, and he is working to prevent it.

Enlightenment matters. Isn't it odd that the general population is being taught to hate the United States? The country itself is very quickly becoming the villain of the story—everyone is choosing to hate the United States and blame it. They say that it is time to dismantle the nation built upon slavery and racism, but the truth is, just about every single country has a similar backstory. Is it okay? No! Racism is not okay—but it also is not the case that we need to completely cannibalize the culture that is developed. It is not the case that we need to destroy the entirety of the nation. The reason that this is happening is that when we are divided, we are easier to control. It is easier to control populations that do not get along. It is easier to control people that do not want to connect together than it is to control people who work separately.

Remember, Q states repeatedly:

"Together, we will win. WWG1WGA!!!"

This is true. We need to unite together. If we want to win and overthrow the corruption that we face, we must make sure that we work together. We must ensure that we are awakened together. We must reject the world around us together, and all of this happens simply enough—you just have to be willing to see past the veils and smoke. Take off those rose-tinted glasses and see the world for what it really is.

The movement is here to help you and people like you to wake up. It is here to show you the atrocities that none of us want to face or admit. It is time to address the people who are doing harm. It is time to face the people who need to remove the blinders. It is time to rip them off and see the patterns that are there. They are no longer coincidences. They are no longer deniable. They want to take control, and they do not care if you or those that you love get hurt. You are nothing but workers—you are the worker ants in the anthill that are expendable and easily replaceable. You are the people that do not matter and never will matter. Your safety and your well-being is not a concern.

Because of this, it is time to prepare for the Storm. We do not know when the Storm will hit or what it will look like. However, as Trump once referenced, there will be a storm, and we have to be ready for it and the aftermath. We are currently in the calm before the storm, but we have to be ready. We have to be willing to fend off the threats that are all around us. We have to be ready to take control and fight. If we can do that, we can thrive.

Remember, everything will make sense in the end. Everything will come together and work together when everything is done. We will see the truth eventually, and while we are getting it in a trickle now, it has to be that way. We have to be eased into the reality of things. We have to get to know what is happening, little by little. We have to recognize that there is a very real consequence of pretending that nothing is happening, and it is time for us to own it.

As you start following Q's posts more often, you will likely begin to see this. You will see that there is more to the picture than you often realize. You will very quickly learn that what you do is what you get, and that is that. If you want to be able to successfully navigate the world around you, you will need to understand what it will take to make it happen.

So, as you head out in the world, it is time for you to start thinking critically. It is time for you to figure out what the truth is. Pay attention to what is said. Watch the news, but do so with scrutiny. Remember that the news is going to censor what is said. The news works to sell you a story, not to report the truth, and because of that, you need to be mindful. There are very few sources for news that are genuine, and you will need to take that into consideration. Despite your teaching in school, it is time for you to recognize that you may need to look outside the box to understand the world around you.

As Q wrote in December of 2019:

"Backchannels are important. Know your history, and you will know why. Q"

Along with:

"The message must bypass MSM"

MSM refers to mainstream media. One source that is commonly pointed to is to go to sources where freedom of speech is still recognized. Sources such as 4chan and 8kun are referred to. In other speeches, President Trump has more clearly stated this: "You know the good news is, at least we have a forum, we have a place we can talk, so everyone knows what is going on."

This references the community on 4chan known as /pol/. This is further supported by General Michael Flynn stating: "And we have an army, 'kay, as a soldier and as a general, as a retired general, we have an army of digital soldiers. What we are now, what we call, what I call them, 'cause this was an insurgency, folks, this was run like an insurgency. This was irregular warfare at its finest, in politics. And that, that story will continue to be told here, but we have what we call citizen journalists, 'kay, because the journalists that we have in our media did a disservice, to themselves actually more than they did to this country. They did a disservice to themselves because they displayed an arrogance that is unprecedented. And so the American people decided to take over the idea of information. They took over the idea of information, and they did it through social media."

As Flynn continues to speak, he says, "He's an American patriot. So when we talk about patriotism, how do we fight as patriots today?" In discussing physical courage and being on the battlefield, he segues into intellectual warfare: "I completely believe the opposite now for our younger generation. And it's the most, the more, the older you get in the military, we sort of begin to change that physical courage to what I call intellectual courage. And intellectual courage actually takes more bravery at times. Takes more bravery at times. Because to be intellectually courageous, and this is for you, this is really for this foundation, this is for the young people in this room, you are, you are demonstrating a level of intellectual courage that our country desperately needs."

What does this mean? It is clear that the Trump admin is referencing that you must be your own news source. He is stating that it is imperative to look to sources that are uncensored if you want the truth. That is the only way that you will ever see the world for what it is supposed to be.

Chapter 10: Q's Reach Around the World

Q's reach is far further than just the United States, even if Q's primary objective at the moment is to clear out the swamp and ensure that justice prevails. However, consider this—Q is trying to eradicate a global operation that would have the entire world living as one unit without any sort of division. This means that the people would not have their separate countries or ethnicities—we would all be one new world and one order that needed to be controlled. Because of this wider-reaching idea and the fact that the current intention is to ensure that the people are not completely subjugated and controlled, Q has gained followers around the world. Although the bulk of the support is within the US, it can be found just about anywhere.

Keep in mind, however, that Qanon is commonly known as terroristic by many mainstream individuals at worst or lacking any sort of rationalization by those in charge. It is the case that the theories here should not be completely disregarded; however—there are many people who are interested in it for a reason. Many people are ready to wake up. They are ready to see the truth and recognize the crimes against humanity that are occurring. There are crimes against children, against adults, against minorities and majorities. The Cult has enemies everywhere—they only care to support and maintain themselves, and they will do anything possible to ensure that it will happen in this manner. It is the case that you will see that these people are going to be exploitative by nature.

Q is quick to remind the world that "We have it all." This is important—it is being noted like this so that the people know that Q is not going to simply try to stake claim to something—they have the information to back up whatever it is that they are trying to push. They have everything that they would need to ensure that they pass what it is that they are looking for, and they will do what they can to make it happen. They will take control in any way possible—they will be able to ensure that they are working with their best ability to ensure that they can and will make certain that they get their way across.

Within this chapter, we are going to take a look at some of the influences that Q has throughout the world and what has been done to try to keep it under wraps. The truth is, Q is everywhere. Though Q's theories are predominantly based in the United States, we must all, no matter the location, work to prevent these problems from happening throughout the world. Do not forget that when we come together, we are powerful, and we can do great things. We must be willing to do so together. We must work together. We must ensure that we do thrive together and that all begins with knowing what it is that Q has to state to us all.

Q in the United States

Q is, for the most part, considered the alt-right side of politics. He is believed to be associated with someone working hard to ensure that the world is enlightened. He has, according to many, been involved with the Trump administration for far longer than many people seem to realize. He is someone that is able to be highly influential around the world. He has been able to ensure that the people know what they are doing—he is meant to show off to the world that he has the knowledge that needs to be passed on, and he expects others to piece it together.

All around the world, people have grown more desperate to understand these strange drops that have happened online. People want to relate to what he is saying or doing. They may even identify with him or praise him for his actions. Signs declaring "WE ARE Q" can be found around the United States, and people who go to Trump rallies may even wear shirts emblazoned with the letter for all to see. People are quick to doubt Q for being little more than conspiracies, but the truth is, he is more than that. He is someone that is more than capable of being scapegoated out— he is someone that is going to be seen as a problem, especially by the mainstream media. People believe that he is lying or someone just trying to have some fun. This is not the case, however—he is actually there trying to help the world. He wants to keep people safe and ensure that they are able to relate to everything.

Because of this, Q is someone who is largely either applauded for what he does or hated and feared for being who he is. The truth is far more complex than that. However, he is someone that is meant to be trusted, and his information must be scrutinized. Remember, Q states that we must question everything and everyone—including Q himself. He wants to create a world of free thinkers—of critical thinkers that will be able to see through the nonsense being fed to them. E wants to ensure that the people are able to recognize that ultimately, there has to be some sort of change.

Thanks to the people becoming more and more radicalized as time has gone by, people have realized that Q is not necessarily as terroristic as people may say. The truth is becoming more and more radicalized. The truth is becoming something that is highly influential. It is something that will set the people free. It is something that you will need, and Q has helped people to see this. The riots of 2020 have been eye-opening to many people. It is easy for people to see that ultimately, there is no way that these riots are not staged. People are becoming more "woke," as they commonly say online, meaning that they see the world for what it is, and they are not afraid to call it out.

Q in Australia

Despite the US orientation, Q has actually gained many supporters in Australia. Globally, Q has become something showing that the whole world will be impacted. These issues are not US-specific—but they will hurt everyone involved if they are not allowed to heal. They will hurt everyone if they are not able to finish working. From questioning the erection of 5G towers during the COVID lockdowns to questioning other theories, people are starting to wonder how much the government is actually telling us and why they are lying about many issues that should be completely disclosed.

In Australia, Q has begun building a following due to the fact that Q encourages enlightenment and education. He pushes people to learn more about the world and to see past the coincidental to recognize that there is more to it than meets the eye. He wants people to understand that what they are doing and seeing will need to be seen. He wants them to recognize the truth: That the government is not always honest and in countries like Australia, where there are certain restrictions on freedoms that can be difficult to muster up. Nevertheless, where there is a will, there is a way, and Q followers are beginning to see this. There are all sorts of reasons that Australians have chosen to latch onto Q and the followers, including:

- Conspiracy theories that one government will be pushed. One way that Q has pushed citizens of Australia to become more radicalized is the idea that the world is being controlled by the elites and that the elites only care about keeping themselves elite and everyone else subservient. This idea was pushed in 1992 by Australian Senator Malcolm Roberts, who asserted that the UN's Agenda 21 plan was meant to actually take over the country. Though initially designed to be sustainable, it was actually going to systematically remove freedoms and sovereignty from the people. Despite the façade that it was meant to push people to be better, the truth is that it actually made people worse. It was the case that people actually became stuck—they would have been controlled and kept under by corrupt individuals that wanted to control everyone involved. Of course, this did not really sit well with Australians, who wanted to maintain their freedom.

- Perceiving that the government would be controlled by pedophiles. One of the biggest points that Q pushes is that these people, meaning the rulers, are sick. The idea that the government would be going around systematically violating and abusing children is terrifying to most people and revolting to just about everyone. Our children are the center of our worlds while we raise them, and the idea that someone would harm them creates a visceral reaction. Many people would not hesitate to kill someone harming their children in front of them, and having their children abused is often one of the parents' worst nightmares. Nevertheless, it is something that must be faced. Of course, the government will not go out to advertise their involvement with this—they will not take the time to tell people that they are actively abusing children or that they are working hard to make children from Haiti disappear a la the Clinton Foundation after the massive earthquake. They are trying to make themselves seem likable, respectable, and innocent in it all. However, when you see pictures of Joe Biden sniffing children or kissing his minor granddaughter, you start to wonder just how much truth is there. For the Australians, the idea is that if we are tasked with protecting our children, then isn't it our duty to completely dismantle and tear down anything that would hurt them— even if what is hurting them is the very government that we are a part of? This is precisely what people do—they tear it down.

- The idea that governments may be unaccountable or incompetent also pushes people more and more extreme as well. We've seen a steady stream of governments that seem to be incompetent or unable to effectively do anything that is necessary to survive or thrive. They flounder and fail, and the people lose all hope or faith in their government as a result. This is not okay by any means—it needs to be fixed somehow, but the way that it is is often not as easy as people believe. Q gives us the idea that we can let go of the idea of an incompetent government. The idea that we can simply reject it and be done with it is highly compelling, and many people will find themselves driven to do so. We see people in Australia and around the world loving this idea of asking for accountability in the government. Remember, the government works for you, not the other way around. The government only has the authority to govern for as long as you give it consent to do so. If the people rejcct that consent aiid no longer allow for it, then the government loses its power. It needs something to back up its claim to power.

- Another common reason that people start to identify more with Q is to step away from governmental corruption, which often supports the idea of big pharma. This is driven forward even more due to the large number of people choosing to step away from vaccines and push for natural healthcare. The idea of natural, alternative methods of treatment over choosing to take medications or drugs that were manmade is highly appealing to others. These people have a natural, inherent sense of doubt for authority and those that they do not believe have their best interests at heart. This has led to a larger amount of people in Australia jumping on the Q bandwagon. This is especially the case after pushes for new vaccines. The idea that the COVID-19 vaccine may become mandatory is terrifying for many, especially because there have been vaccine programs where vaccines were mandated and shortly after, women were left sterile in Africa. They were medically sterilized by the vaccines that they were being given without any choice. They were told that they needed the vaccines and that they would keep them healthy—but this also caused them to run into other issues that would need to be addressed as well.

- Finally, the idea that COVID-19 has been highly weaponized is appealing to the Australians. The common debate that you can see sprinkled across Q's posts are that the coronavirus was not actually as big of a deal as people made it out to be. The idea is that COVID-19 would have been no big deal and that the death rates are far lower than people seem to think or than what are being reported. This idea of overreporting helps to keep people under control. People who are scared are people who are complacent and will allow the people to do whatever they want with them. They are willing to sacrifice their freedoms to ensure that they continue to get what they want or need and in this case, it would be to avoid getting ill. But, as more and more people start to believe that COVID-19 is no big deal, it is the case that Q, who says that this is nothing more than an attempt to control the people during the election year to prevent a victory for Trump, becomes more popular—even outside of the world. When the whole world is lying to create and maintain this idea of a "plandemic" it becomes the case that you are likely to start doubting everything.

Q Followers around the World

No matter the locale, however, Q followers typically will share a few key characteristics that help to make them a bit more willing to believe what is being pushed to them. They see the information in front of them and want to work with it. They want to become more.

They want to find that justice in the world that they believe ought to be out there. Most Q followers will follow a few traits, such as:

1. Unhappiness. Many of those that are following Q is currently displeased with the state of the government, the world, and those around them. They need to be able to go against those around them. Think of those who are angry or frustrated with the pandemic. They do not like what they are currently facing. They do not enjoy the lockdowns or the way that the economy is crashing. They are unwilling to stand by and allow the whole world to be dismantled, little by little. They want more. They want better for themselves and the people around them. Q gives them hope for that. Q reminds them that they are able to do better if they question the government—if they push for change. Q is quick to remind the people that the government works for them, not the other way around. When all of those governmental complaints

are revealed by Q over time, people naturally begin to take notice. They naturally figure out what it will take for them to take control, and that usually aligns with the following Q.

2. Many of Q's followers have overlapping social circles. This is even truer now that we've got the internet that makes connecting with other people that share beliefs easier than ever. If you want to be able to talk to people who share your beliefs, the forms are a Google search away, and you will likely find someone that will match up with your beliefs as well. This means that it becomes than ever to surround yourself with people that also have similar beliefs.

3. Political reasons. Q has very specific, largely conservative belief systems. Q pushes for people to remember when America was great—a time when religion and pride in one's country mattered. Patriotism was largely important to Q—and is pushed regularly. Q pushes this often with statements such as

"God Bless America" or "Patriots" and the like. Those who feel strongly that the nation should be something to be proud to find that oftentimes, they feel like patriotism has gone out the window, and they want to get it back somehow. They want to figure out how they can return to their own patriotic roots, and Q provides a method for doing so.

The Mainstream Response to Q

Of course, the mainstream media is doing everything in its power to silence Q and prevent any of this information from coming forth. If you've watched the news recently, you've seen several attempts to silence Q and Q followers, stating that it is a conspiracy theory. It is commonly lumped in with the people who believe that the earth is flat or other similar tales. There are headlines all over the news such as "The Qanon Conspiracy" or "Qanon: A Threat to Democracy and Rationality." These titles do not bode well for Q or the followers.

But, this attempt to discredit Q is not working nearly as well as they may hope.

Think about it—if Q were not a real threat, would they really be getting the same sort of backlash? No one cared about the people believing in Flat Earth Theories. No one cared other than to look at the occasional story that made the people look uneducated, such as trying to fly up high enough to see the curvature of the earth or stating that there is an edge to the earth somewhere despite the photographic evidence showing otherwise. Those believing in flat earth do not get the same media attention that Q does.

This is because the media is threatened. The media is concerned that Qanon's theory will go mainstream. They know that if everyone believes what Q is saying, the guise is up. Everything will fall apart and crumble to the ground, and that is not very appealing to anyone. The more that Q gains a following, the more desperate people become. The more desperate the media becomes, the more fervently they will try to silence Q.

If there were no truth to it, they would not care. They would not say a word about they would not bother trying to silence it because there would be no harm in it. Nevertheless, here we are—there are people in power that should not be, and if Q is correct and people start to agree with that sentiment, then the Left will lose everything.

Of course, there have been some serious changes made to attempt to silence Q and prevent those from discussing the theories themselves. There are people out there who wholeheartedly want to ensure that no one can speak in these manners, and they've taken control of media and social media. Let's look at a few of these reactions:

- **Reddit bans Qanon subreddits:** Subreddits are the individual boards that people can post on within the site. They are commonly themed with names that will tell you what you can expect to see or get form that particular board. Some are filled with people talking about cooking, cheering people up, television shows, politics, and you guessed it—Qanon theory. Or at least, up until recently, they did. Nowadays, there is a blanket ban on Qanon related subreddits. Some of the most popular ones have all been eradicated and banned from the site. Reddit cites that they did so because the boards violated the terms and conditions of the site by inciting violence. They have now made it impossible to share this information in this manner. This was one of the best places to go to discuss the information that would not involve going to 4chan or 8kun, which may weed out several people who cannot tolerate the kind of language that is used on those sources. Nevertheless, with that blanket ban on Q related information, Reddit is no longer a safe place to go

- **Facebook and Instagram remove Qanon posts and groups:** Facebook and Instagram have also both restricted posts related to Q. Commonly, these groups related to Q are censored and blocked from showing up in the recommendations fo the site. They block people from being invited. However, they were not banned completely. Several groups and accounts directly related to Qanon theories have also been banned, especially as they started popping up more and more.

- **Twitter removing Qanon accounts:** Twitter jumped on the bandwagon as well, removing over 7000 accounts believed to relate to Qanon theory. They also stated that they would ban discussion of Qanon entirely from Twitter due to the fact that they believed that it was harmful. They claimed that the Qanon information would cause problems off the internet, and they believed that those who would discuss the information would do more harm than good, and therefore, they deserved to be silenced and censored. So much for free speech. Across Twitter, Qanon can no longer trend, and over 150,000 accounts were banned and blocked out from sharing this information.

- **Google censoring searches:** If you're curious about this one, try searching for information about Qanon on Google. The search engine has censored it to allow for information to be buried. This means that much of the information that you will see about Qanon is going to be negative if you use a source such as Google. They use search engine optimization, and it became simple to manipulate it just right to ensure that the people are able to bury the information entirely. This means that if you want to be able to get Qanon information, you will have to know how to look for it. You will need to go to search engines such as DuckDuckGo that are not censored in the same way.
- **YouTube censoring videos:** Though YouTube has not been completely eradicating all of the information found on their site, they have been cracking down on what is allowed to trend and what cannot. And, if you were to look

up Qanon on YouTube, you would discover that there is a warning displayed showing you what Qanon is and then showing you the information that they want you to see—and that is primarily negative.

- **Removal of sites dedicated to congregating information:** Lately, several sites that have traditionally pulled together posts by Q and provided them for easy access for people to see everything in order or to search through them have been banned or shut down. Qmap.pub was the first to go—the site was closed after the owner of the site, Jason Gelinas, was outed by Logically.ai and claimed that they were able to connect the site to his home address. He did not confirm or deny the truth but stated that he was staying uninvolved. As a result, he recently lost his job at Citigroup. Other sites are similarly under attack by people attempting to tear down the information. The world does not want you to know about Qanon theory—they want to hide the information and prevent you from ever having to see it. After all, if you see it, it might make too much sense and cause problems for you if you were to fall for it.

These attempts to shut down Q from the internet are blatant—they are there to prevent you from being able to learn the truth and form being able to acknowledge what matters to you. They are there to cause issues for you when it comes to an understanding what you want or need. These issues matter. These issues are relevant to just about everyone. They ought to be paid attention to.

Conclusion

And that brings us to the end of this book. Are you ready? Do you have a better understanding of everything that you will need to know at this point in time? Do you feel better knowing that you have the knowledge to start figuring out what matters and how to navigate throughout the world? Hopefully, you feel much more confident and ready to make your own decisions. The best thing that you can hope for in your time reading through this material is that you do feel more justified and empowered in questioning the world around you. You should feel like questioning what is happening is the right way to go.

Remember, the whole purpose of this book was not to indoctrinate you or force you to think, act, or vote a certain way. This book, was meant to introduce you to the theories pushed by Q, and those theories are meant to teach you to think for yourself. What you need more than anything is to make sure that you are willing and able to think for yourself so you can live for yourself. If you can do that, you will thrive, but it all begins with that willingness to see past nonsense.

You cannot just blindly trust whatever you see out there. Question everything. Find good sources. Question biases. Be willing to stand up for what is right. If you can do this, you will be more successful. You just have to know what you are doing and how. From here on out, you are tasked with remembering to question it all. You are tasked with ensuring that you are on track. Make sure that you pay closer attention and figure out what it will take for you to do your part.

Justice will prevail. The corruption will be ousted, and we can drain the swamp known as the Deep State. All we have to do is stick to it and see the truth. Let other people see the truth as well. Be open-minded to corruption. Allow yourself to see that corruption and question it. Remind yourself that you will need to do this to properly process everything. Make sure that you scrutinize it all and figure out what it will take.

Thank you for taking control of this book. Hopefully, as you read through, you felt like the information that you have gained was highly influential and eye-opening. Hopefully, you feel more enlightened and more convinced of the truth—whatever the truth is for you. If you thought that this book was influential for you, then please consider heading over to Amazon and leaving a review.

And remember, we will prevail. When we work together, we are stronger than we think. When we work together and remain undivided, we can succeed and thrive. It is time for you to think about what you will need to do. And remember: WWG1WGA!

Description

Have you heard about Qanon on television or in the news recently and been curious about what it is? Are you wondering what's behind this strange theory and want to know more about it? If so, then keep reading... This book is for you!

Within this book, we are going to address the truth. And that truth can be difficult for many people to stomach. If you are someone who has always sat idly and believed everything that you read online, then you are probably precisely who should be targeted in this book. When you read through this book, you will be learning about Qanon from the perspective of believers for potential believers. As you read through this book, you will learn all about what you need.

In particular, as you read, you will be guided through how to understand Q, the posts that Q makes, and why people follow this theory. You will learn about what makes it so incredibly compelling for all of those who choose to follow it, and that is greatly beneficial to you. You will learn exactly why this movement is sweeping across the world, even with people trying left and right to prevent it from gaining traction.

Q wants you to be informed. He wants you to know what is happening in the world around you, and he wants you to see through the blatant lies that mainstream media is trying to force-feed you.

If you're ready to learn the truth, then this book is for you and it's time for you to get started! Within these pages, you will get truths such as:

- The meaning of the phrase "Where We Go One, We Go All" and why it matters
- Where Q resides and what he posts
- The most common Qanon themes that you will need to understand
- What the New World Order is and why you need to care
- Information about how close President Trump is to Q and why people believe that they are working together

- Who is playing in the Qanon game and what the roles they play are
- How to begin to understand Q and how he posts, including learning about tripcodes, deltas, and some explanations of the most common phrases he uses
- How Q communicates and some of the biggest, most compelling drops of information that Q has made
- How to understand why Q is insistent that Obama was a shadow president and how they are trying to get control again
- What the goal of Q is and how to get to it
- How far Q has reached around the world
- What the mainstream media is doing to combat Q
- *AND MORE*

If you are ready to start understanding it all from the top to the bottom to better recognize what it is that you will need to understand, then what are you waiting for? Scroll up and click on BUY NOW to begin learning all about Q, Q's theories, and why they matter. The sooner you can take off your blinders and see the world, the better.